One Voice

Helene King

authorHOUSE®

AuthorHouse™ UK Ltd.
500 Avebury Boulevard
Central Milton Keynes, MK9 2BE
www.authorhouse.co.uk
Phone: 08001974150

First published by AuthorHouse 7/27/2009

ISBN: 978-1-4389-9921-0 (sc)

This book is printed on acid-free paper.

Contents

FOREWORD   1

ACKNOWLEDGEMENTS   3

CHAPTER ONE ONE VOICE   5

An invitation to listen for THE VOICE – the voice of God once known in childhood, but lost in the clamour of inner voices which we accumulate as we grow into adulthood. The VOICE has planted in us dreams, which may be lost, but can be recovered - even among the young people of Citylife.

Appreciating the journey of life as a journey of faith in God's generosity, illustrated with stories from Citylife. The journey becomes a pilgrimage of discovery of God's goodness in creation, discovering God's pathway beneath our feet.

CHAPTER TWO ARE WE NEARLY THERE YET?   16

A sore heart makes us afraid to dream and keeps us "living on the outside" rather than facing the inner pain. We recognise the plight of the elder brother who failed to know he was loved by his father. Questions of the heart in the rucksack for the journey.

CHAPTER THREE MY TUMMY'S SORE   30

A sore heart makes us afraid to dream and keeps

us "living on the outside" rather than facing the inner pain. We recognise the plight of the elder brother who failed to know he was loved by his father. Questions of the heart in the rucksack for the journey.

CHAPTER FOUR SAY MY NAME   41

We all need to be noticed, but does God even know my name? A desperate prayer and the very public recognition as Childline Woman of the Year. A dream of a white horse and an invitation to adventure with God. Listening again to THE VOICE.

The experience of abandonment with poignant stories of home. The orphan spirit described in personal terms and recognised in our culture. Contrasted with the freedom of knowing we are sons and daughters of our heavenly Father.

CHAPTER FIVE ALL BY MYSELF   52

The life-transforming experience of being a "son of God" following years of preparation for the moment through years of Bible study. The vital importance of living in the 'grace and peace' of God, and then living it out by learning contentment and by showing God's generosity and justice in today's world.

CHAPTER SIX YOU'LL NEVER WALK ALONE   64

The life-transforming experience of being a "son of God" following years of preparation for the moment through years of Bible study. The vital importance of living in the 'grace and peace' of God, and then living it out by learning contentment and by showing God's generosity and justice in today's world.

CHAPTER SEVEN WE ARE FAMILY 77

Community begins in God. As society breaks apart the rise in loneliness and depression creates a hunger of genuine community. Citylife becomes a family – a place of belonging led by a team of committed people.

CHAPTER EIGHT HEART FOR THE YOUNG 87

Early beginnings of compassion for children and later connections through faithful contact with families. Fear, authority and love. The need for stability and rhythm in life. Stories of long term work with individuals as ancient prophecy is fulfilled.

The experiences of the years are passed on to leaders to live the freedom of God's children, and to face up to the inner hurts which result in authoritarian leadership. How do we lead others into this freedom unless first we receive it and live in it?

CHAPTER NINE AN INVITATION TO LEADERS 102

The experiences of the years are passed on to leaders to live the freedom of God's children, and to face up to the inner hurts which result in authoritarian leadership. How do we lead others into this freedom unless first we receive it and live in it?

About the Author 113

FOREWORD

If you want to understand what Jesus meant about the sheep knowing his "voice" and following his "voice", then read this story of Helene King and Citylife.

One woman began with one little girl. The Voice of the Good Shepherd led her to care for this one girl – one lamb to be fed and nurtured. Other children followed. She tried to bring them into the fold of the church, but these children were too boisterous and too disturbed for the orderly world of church.

She listens to the Voice. She stays with her little flock. Another fold is needed to protect and provide for them. She does not set out to build a church. She simply follows the Voice to care for these children.

Twenty years later she has mothered many troubled youngsters into the Father heart of God. In a shop unit on the edge of one of Edinburgh's housing estates, a little family of God's children has grown up. To visit them feels like visiting the underground church – below the radar of official statistics and church projects.

The jargon and debates about emerging church sound hollow alongside this account of relentless compassion, flowing from the deep intimacy of being a child of a Father who is generous and hospitable beyond words.

There is a rawness about this story. There is an unpolished honesty. There is an unsophisticated style. Listen for the heartbeat beneath the broken speech rhythms of the writing. It is a heart beating in time with the heart of God, inviting us to listen to the Voice and to follow where He will lead.

The Good Shepherd said: "I have other sheep that are not of this sheep pen. I must bring them also. They too will listen to my voice and there will be one flock and one shepherd." (John 10: 16)

The plea of this book is for more communities of healing love where broken children of our time will find spiritual fathers and mothers to point them to the Father-heart of God made know to us through Jesus Christ.

Reverend Peter Neilson

Lent 2009

ACKNOWLEDGEMENTS

To my son Alan and family for their patience, love and support as I have tried to find out how to be a mum and a grandma while struggling with orphan issues.

To the Core Team of Citylife

To Fiona Cain who helped me with the chapter titles, but more for her compassion and love for the young and her heart of intercession.

To Graeme Mackel for his steadfastness and his sense of humour when things get too serious.

To Ian Dyson for his service to Citylife and his desire to shape it and for his heart for the oppressed.

To Julia Mackel, who is right behind me (only you know what that means), for her desire to see the Father's love being revealed in order that the purposes of God can be fulfilled in people's lives.

To Mark Pecqueur for his prophetic voice and years of experience but also for his heart for the widow (namely me) and the orphan.

To Tim Cain for his apostolic calling and giving me the push I needed to follow my heart.

My thanks and love for the family at Citylife who have helped to form a community of believers working together to see transformation take place. Thank you for being His arms around me.

To Fatherheart Ministries whose revelation of a father, who is loving me right now, was beyond my wildest dreams.

Lastly to the Rev Peter Neilson whose gifting with people helped draw out from me more than I knew that I had, and for his patience in editing and shaping the book. Thank you.

All proceeds from this book go to Citylife. Citylife charity no SC031375   info@citylifeonline.org   www.citylifeonline.org

CHAPTER ONE
ONE VOICE

One Voice among Many

I begin this story with a question. Why write a book?

There are so many books and even King Solomon says that 'too many books weary the mind'. However, I pray that this book will touch your heart as well as your mind.

The answer to my own question is a response to the number of prophetic words that had been given to me that I have A VOICE with something to say; and that I might also be A VOICE TO THOSE WHO HAVE NO VOICE.

This book is entitled ONE VOICE because I am so aware that many VOICES clamour for our attention. The world is such a noisy place filled with such a volume of sound that sometimes it is difficult to be heard.

Many young people in Citylife Ministries where I am the pastor cannot go to sleep without an MP3 player on, a mobile phone lying on the pillow beside their head, or falling asleep with the television on. In the houses that I visit there is a confusion of noise, children and adults all shouting at one for one very simple reason - they want to be heard.

However, I think that the INNER VOICES shout louder than any of the other VOICES. When one young girl told me she couldn't sleep without music playing, I asked her 'Is it because you can't handle the little voices inside?' She laughed and said. 'Oh yes!'

These INNER VOICES are the ones that form and direct our lives, but there is ONE VOICE only that needs to be heard. How do I learning to listen to that ONE VOICE more than any other? When I do, I have the grace to respond to other people's VOICES and even have the courage to listen to my own.

In childhood I believed I heard that VOICE which gave me such a freedom and joy and childlike trust as I danced around the trees in the meadows. I was always aware of that VOICE until the weight of life and the urge to grow up and be mature took hold of me.

Voices of Childhood

The first audible VOICES that I heard were naturally from my own mother and father. My mother's VOICE was always gentle and encouraging. In my late teens and early twenties she would be there to greet me after an evening out. She would have on my favourite record on, a flask of tea for the two of us to share and dainty little triangles sandwiches to munch on as she showed her interest in my comings and goings sitting on the end of my bed. Much later I discovered she had been brought up in a children's home and not in a boarding school as she had always said. This had a marked effect on all her relationships and she was inclined to withdraw into herself. When you cannot reveal who you really are, you become very lonely and you live in a world all by yourself.

The other VOICE I heard was from my father. He was kind in his own way, but he was a bit of a snob and he cared more about what people thought than about us kids. He wanted us to do well at school. That is not a bad thing, but I believe it was so that we could look good in the eyes of other people. This attitude instilled in my brother and sisters and me a striving to please which brings exhaustion and a feeling of never making the mark.

My father carried with him an air of authority. He had a good job in the Civil Service and because of his role he always had to wear a suit and he carried an air that to a degree, made him unapproachable.

Tim is a great friend and one of the Core Group of Citylife, but in the early days of establishing Citylife I used to be uncomfortable during discussions as we set up our ministry. Now Tim is nothing like my dad. Tim is a lot younger, but he wore a suit and carried a position in his occupation. Why did I feel uncomfortable around him? I came to understand that he reminded me of my father. He had an air of authority because of his job. My being uncomfortable with Tim was nothing to do with Tim as a person it was who he represented to me.

We all have filter systems. Dad's suit was pat of my filter system. When we are uncomfortable with someone, often it is not about them, but who they represent to us.

Please understand that I loved my mum and dad. What I have described is not said to pick flaws with them, but our childhood really starts us on our life's journey. I honour my mum and dad. They gave me what they had to give. You cannot give to someone what you have not first received yourself. I honour them because they gave me a great gift. The gift of life.

It is not until we get older that we realize that who we are today is shaped by who we have been. The little girl who was hurt with sharp words and a distant mum ends up becoming part of our core belief, and these early years begin to form our lives, unless the ONE VOICE speaks words of comfort that begin a process of healing and move us on in life.

This insight in my childhood may help you understand the ways of healing and restoration that God brought to my life as I sought throughout the years to hear the ONE VOICE.

St Augustine wrote about that VOICE:

The whole bible does nothing but tell of God's love.....If the written word of the Bible could be changed into a spoken word and become one single VOICE, this VOICE more powerful that the roaring of the sea, would cry out. 'The Father loves you' (Jn 16:27).

The question is: How can we respond to God's cry if our frame of reference for a father comes through our own earthly father?

The Voice and the Dream

As a little girl, I had a dream of giving to the poor. I dreamed it, and my imagination ran with it, but I did not recognise where it came from. I did not recognise that at an early age the Kingdom of God was being placed within me. My heart's desire is to see the Kingdom of God come into the community where I live, because I have come to understand that the Kingdom of God is not like the world's system of buying and selling, but about giving and receiving, knowing God's love for me and giving it away to the next person I meet.

I want MY VOICE to sound, not like a hollow cavern, but to have a ring of life to it.

I want it to beat with one rhythm, one sound, and to have ONE VOICE. As I speak, THAT VOICE will reverberate on the wings of the wind. It will start in a whisper 'I LOVE YOU' growing louder and louder until it shouts, when the groaning of creation stops as the sons of God are revealed on the earth (Romans 8:19-20)

I believe that there is a dream inside each one of us, a dream that causes us to get out of bed in the morning. Someone said that 'the limitations of your dreams are the limitations of your life.' W B Yeats said that to lose your dream is to lose yourself – the most important part of yourself. If you have lost that perhaps you are dead.

Losing the VOICE

Maybe it is because I am growing older, but I have been thinking about what it was like when I was a child and the aliveness I felt in my soul. I would spend my days as a child skipping, dancing and singing – weaving my way in and out of the trees in the meadows giggling and laughing at the joy of being alive.

Until recently most of that feeling had been dying. The dying inside had been subtle and gradual. It was the beginning of little deaths of dreams and visions and even the joy of living.   Playing and dancing through the trees wasn't the point. It was the fact of being really alive.   It was the VOICE I heard deep inside, a warm and loving VOICE, a believing VOICE, a wild and dangerous voice that came as I danced through the trees. I began to recognise this VOICE as a VOICE that said, 'I believe in you'. When you hear that VOICE often enough, you begin to believe in yourself, and begin to believe the fulfilment of the dream within. Perhaps it is not the fulfilment that is important but the moving onwards within the dream.

THE VOICE said, "You can learn to fly." THE VOICE said, "You can do something great. You can do whatever your heart desires. I've put a dream in you." Every time I heard that VOICE, I recognized who it was – it was the VOICE of God. Not until many years later did I realize who it really was – the VOICE of my heavenly Father.

Recovering the VOICE

There is deep within all of us – a VOICE. It speaks to us continuously, knocking on the door of our heart. When we are kids, that VOICE is very familiar. This VOICE has an excitement and a thrill to it. When we hear it, it causes us to gasp with a joy we cannot understand. Its loudness is not like a thunder. It shouts to us with a whisper deep inside. It is like the wind blowing on our faces, like a kiss from the beloved awakening us up, like the prince coming to Sleeping Beauty, causing her to stir and awaken.

It is the VOICE of our childhood and it is the VOICE of wonder and amazement – the voice of God which has always been speaking to us.

Why do I work with kids at my age? Maybe I am trying to show them – in the loudness and violence and lostness of their childhood – the wonder of childhood, the real teaching of Jesus, who said, 'Unless you become like a child, you cannot enter the Kingdom of God' (Matthew 18). Maybe I am trying to bring to these kids a sense of awe and wonder of a life touched by Jesus.

When I was about eight years old I remember the tremendous excitement of the school holidays and the decisions I had to make: to play hopscotch on the pavement outside the house, or to kick around in the back garden, or to go to the park and play hide and seek, or swing on the swings so high with the strong belief that if I swung high enough my toes would reach the puffy white clouds. I was so sure I could fly.

Then one sad day we come to realise that we cannot hear the VOICE. We can't fly, and so the dream of reaching the sky dies. We no longer hear the VOICE of God in that infinite way again, and our soul becomes dull.

However, I can sense that I am about to embark on a new way of living, embarking on a life of adventure, and I know that if I listen to the VOICE in my heart, this VOICE will lead me into danger that excites and stimulates.

Where this VOICE will lead, the scared ones cannot go. The religious cannot go there. The ones who are comfortable with this world's system cannot go. But this VOICE beckons. This VOICE calls. This VOICE does not demand but invites. Again and again this VOICE says,– 'Come'. Jesus often said, 'Come. Follow Me'. This invitation is not like a command to a dog 'come for a walk'. This is an invitation to be so at one with Him that where He goes you find yourself with Him. He will lead me into dangerous territory. There will be new things to experience, a place where every day will be an experience of thrills and wonder.

I am discovering something that I have always known - something which leads me to do what I do with the kids. My story – and I am only on the tip of discovering it - is all about the attributes of children that make childhood an adventure. This is where adults rediscover these shrivelled up remnants of dreams and creativity, and rediscover ourselves - our real selves, the persons we were made to be. When we are grown up, mature 'got it all together' people, we come to realise that we don't have it all together after all. Deep inside we are really just children, who are asked to respond to our Father   When we come to that place, we find ourselves. We find our dreams again. We find that we are dancing again, but to a different rhythm. When we begin to find this, we find ourselves.

Lost and Found

I do not understand how we find ourselves on the treadmill of life. Instead of leading us deeper into hearing the VOICE inside of us, it takes us further and further away. The busyness and demands of life pull us away, and we begin to lose our LIFE – the LIFE that causes every cell in our body to respond with an aliveness and a joy that makes us giggle and laugh like children without even knowing why.

What happened? What happened to our aliveness? How could we grow up, accumulate twelve years of education, get married, have kids, work for decades and never really live.   The death of the soul is never quick. It is a slow dying, a succession of little deaths that continues until we wake up one day on the boundary of God's VOICE - on the fringe of God's love, beyond this adventure of God's claim on our lives.

Nonetheless, today I believe God is at work in all of us who will stay still enough to listen. I believe He is awakening the dream that He and He alone has put within us. When we claim back our childlikeness we stumble upon the Presence of God, and we are amazed to find the place all children know about - the place I knew as a child - dancing through the meadows - the place where we once again can hear the whisper of Jesus.

Jesus always recognised children because they always recognised Him. This is the place where our souls come to life and we sense that we are on the brink of a great and mysterious way of life.

The beginnings of my adventure are not about a list of principles or rules about how to live a happy Christian life. My words are broken and stuttering. They are tiny attempts to describe what I am only relearning - the adventure of a childlike faith.

Like my kids in Kid's Church, my thoughts are messy and disorderly, and far from neat and tidy. My thoughts and words are not articulate or well structured, and not ordered with great grammar. Some of them, like my kids in Kid's Church may be irritating and annoying at times. I ask you to be patient with me as my life and story unfold, because underneath all that is messy, is a life and energy that I want us all to enjoy. Bear with me because I am finding out that there is the possibility of discovery just beyond irritation and chaos.

My spiritual director said to me when we were discussing Kid's Church and the chaos of noisy, unruly and broken kids, 'Helene, don't you think that God can work through chaos and bring a new kind of order'? That question brought another question to my heart. Do I believe that? If I do not have faith in Him, then nothing will happen.

James Jordan of Fatherheart Ministries always says, 'You can have whatever you believe for'. I believe that. I am a bit like that man in Mark chapter 9 who said, 'Lord, I believe, help my unbelief'. In reality, however, I do believe it or else I would give up. Everyday I am learning to say, 'The Lord is here. His Spirit is with us'. When I say that, faith leaps within me. If He is here, working in and through chaos, then His Presence can accomplish more than I can ever begin to understand.

If only we will stay still enough to listen, because the VOICE is quiet. This VOICE does not shout or scream to be heard. Only those who are quiet inside can hear this VOICE because this VOICE speaks in a whisper. This VOICE will reawaken the dream that has been put inside you.

In his book, 'Before We Say Goodbye, Ray Simpson tells this story:

'Chris Evans was dying, leaving behind a husband and an eleven year old son. I recall her saying something like this to me: I don't know exactly what is coming next. But throughout my life I have listened to a VOICE deep inside me, and whenever I have followed this VOICE I have found that there is a response which makes me believe that the world is, at heart, a friend.'□

We become like the object or person we focus on. The woman in Ray Simpson's story focused on the VOICE of God that was deep within. At the end of her life, all that was required of her was to listen to the VOICE that was so familiar to her. She could trust that VOICE even at the end of her physical life.

Martin Luther King famously said, 'I have a dream'. Our Father in His great goodness is looking for us to rekindle his dream. He has been searching for me and He is searching for you. Sometimes it feels as though we are searching for Him, but that does not matter. What does matter is that we meet. Nothing else is important.

The secret of the Christian life is never to grow up because only children can enter the kingdom of God. Only children need a Father. A big grown up person who relies on his own strengths has no need of a Father or even of God. But in our Father's eyes we are all children.

CHAPTER TWO
ARE WE NEARLY THERE YET?

Boredom and Imagination

Taking a group of children from Citylife Ministries out for a day to an adventure park one summer, we started our journey with great excitement. The children discussed what rides they would go on, who they would go with, what was in their picnic bag? There was a lot of noise and chatter.

Five minutes down the road comes the question. 'Are we nearly there yet?' There is still excitement but a sense of impatience and fidgeting.

After half an hour you can almost hear the whingeing as the question is asked again. 'Are we nearly there yet?' The loud chatter of voices has died down a little as they sit clasping their little picnic bag. 'I'm hungry, can I eat my lunch now?' But it is only 11 in the morning.

One little seven year old girl is from a very damaged background. Her mum tries to work hard in order to keep the family together, but she is left to be looked after by the other older children in her family. She always has this lost look in her eyes. She often stands alone. When she is asked to sit down she will move her seat to the middle of the aisle, where no one can pass her, just to be noticed. But her little lost cry is always saying the same thing week after week 'I'm bored'. I don't think she is bored with what is happening at Kid's Church because it has a fast moving programme with multimedia and movement songs and games. I think she is bored with life.

How sad is that? Seven years of age and bored with life. On our journey to an adventure park she struggles to connect. I believe that she is not sure that we really are on a journey to somewhere. She knows she is on the bus, but her little damaged heart cannot accept the fact that she is going somewhere special. For children with nothing to do for a few minutes, they seem to think hours have passed. 'Are we nearly there yet?'

I hear my name called from someone at the front of the bus. 'Helene, are we nearly there yet'? And so I talk about the adventure park - the slides, the flying fox, and all the other activities that are in the park and try to build up a bit of excitement, to take away the boredom. 'And down from the adventure play area there are some little lambs, a pony that you can stroke, and hens trotting about', I say, putting intonation into my voice to capture their imaginations. Then I hear my name calling me from the back of the bus 'Helene, are we nearly there yet'? I repeat the same thing trying to turn their attention to the destination. The destination has become the all-important thing, but they are missing the fun of the journey. They like the singing, the chatter, the scenery that they are passing, but they are still impatient. They want to arrive.

They are beginning to wonder, 'Is there really a destination?' Are we really taking them to where we said we were going?

Help ourselves or Trust in God

How like us in our Christian walk. We hear and read the promises of God and we start off with great excitement, but as the years go by it seems that just like the children, we lose our excitement and the journey becomes a bit mundane and tedious. And we ask the same question again and again as the children did – 'Are we nearly there yet?' We seem to have the idea that we have an arrival point. If we follow the twelve steps on becoming an overcoming Christian, when we master the twelfth, we have arrived. We've made it.

I met with a friend from Citylife who is struggling with her job and the relationships within the company she works for. We talked over a meal together and she told me that her bookshelf at home is full of books on 'How to do this, or how to do that', so many self-help books, She is exhausted trying to apply all these principles to her life. The difficulty for her is how to accept by faith that God has done it all. All she needs is to become a little girl that needs to be loved. It is really not complicated. After I shared with her for a period of time she asked a question that spoke volumes: 'How do I do it'? You do nothing, absolutely nothing. Become a child who needs a Father and let Him do it for you. Let Him carry you. Only children can enter the kingdom of God. A big grown up person has little need of a father, or even of God. Perhaps that is why this world has such a strong independent spirit. 'I can do it all by myself. I have no need of anybody. So we have created a nation of people that do not want help from anybody, and people become very private.

We try so hard to be overcomers, but the fact is we are overcomers because of what Christ has done. When the emphasis is on the fact that we have to get it accomplished, it can be about striving and guilt. When we realise who He is, we want to be like Him and He changes us by prayer, not by our striving to reach a goal. It is the response of love because we love who He is. The more we see how God has laid down His life for others, the more we want to lay down our life; and in laying down our life we find it.

When we become Christians, it seems that we can't stop reading the Bible, because we want to know what God is like. If we are told we must read our Bible, and to have a quiet time we move into legalism. When we are told that we have to be more generous in our giving, the joy goes out of giving.

Tithing and Generosity

I remember tithing to a ridiculous level because I so wanted to do what was right. However, one day God said to me to 'stop' my financial giving to the Church and that I should give it to my son and his family. I believe in giving to the Church, I believe in giving to God, even extravagantly. How can you not give to the One who has given you everything? However, I believe when God told me to stop, it was to show me something of His character.

When God told me to give to my family, I felt impressed by Him to take my family where I had taken young people on a trip to Canada. One lovely summer evening sitting outside a log cabin by a lake in Ontario I spoke to my son and asked him to forgive me for being so involved in ministry when he was younger, rather than being with him. He accepted my apology and something invisible that had been between us disappeared. There was no visible barrier, but you can often sense something in your spirit.

When we came back from our holiday I had a series of smashed windows in my home and my car was broken into twice. I wondered for a brief moment, if I had opened myself up to enemy attack by stopping giving financially to the work of God, but I still had the strong feeling that giving to my son instead of the church had been the right thing to do.

A few weeks later a friend from overseas phoned me and said, 'Helene, I have been thinking about you and I just wondered if there was anything on your heart that you would like to do'. I said that I would love to go to a Fatherheart School which was to be held a month later in the south of England. 'I would like to send you a gift of £1,000 for your flight, fees and accommodation,' he said. I was overcome with John's generosity, and the goodness of God. I realised that if I had started giving to the church again out of guilt, or because I felt I had come out from the covering of God, then, when John's gift came, I would have thought that it I had accomplished something by 'doing the right thing.' God wanted to give to me out of His abundance because I was His child. He loved me whether I gave or not.

During the week at the School I felt on my heart that I should give away the £1,000 I had been given because I had received so much during the teaching and the revelation of who God was for me in my heart. When our hearts are touched by God's extravagance, how can we not give? This taught me a valuable lesson. Now I give because I cannot stop giving, for one simple reason I love Him so much. If I have two coats and my brother has none, I have to give him one of mine because if I say I love God, but see my brother in need how can the love of God be in me? However, the weight of having to give has gone and now I have the joy of giving, because it is more blessed to give than to receive. I want to be like my elder brother, Jesus Christ, who gave His life as a sacrifice for me.

James Jordan says that living in the Kingdom of God is about 'growing down, not growing up'. If it depends on our competency, then we are missing it. We are just children. The Kingdom of God is not about competency and arrival; it is about laying down our lives to the point of death. Love is where we lay down our lives for another.

Jesus Christ, the Son of God said 'I can do nothing of Myself'. Jesus was totally reliant on His Father's Presence in His life to accomplish anything.

It is not about arrival; it is about being on the road.

There is something in our humanity that wants to be strong, to get rid of weakness and to have no problems. We are told to get our act together. However, as James Jordan says, 'Even if you do get your act together, it will still just be an act'.

God is leading us on a pathway to become comfortable with weakness. We are not talking of sin here because sin separates us from God, but about learning to embrace our weaknesses. Paul says, 'When I am weak, then I am strong'.

This journey has one purpose and one destination and it is to go deeper and deeper into the very heart of who God is.   At Kids Church we sing 'God is so Big'. If that is true, then how can there ever be an arrival point.   He is so huge and mysterious that it is silly to think in our tiny little minds that we have mastered the soul of the universe.   This universe and its heartbeat is all the heartbeat of God.   How can there ever be an arrival point to fully grasp the One who is infinite. The One whom even the heavens and the earth cannot contain.   God said to David, a king of Israel in the Old Testament, 'Your son can build a temple, but you cannot contain Me in it.'

Journey or Pilgrimage

"The wheels on the bus go round and round" is one of the songs the children love to sing when we go on trips.   I love it, because it kind of puts a harmony into the journey.   There is a rhythm as they sing, 'The wheels on the bus go round and round, round and round....all day long.'

The song make me ponder as the wheels on the bus pound the tarmac road, 'Is there a pathway below this journey?

In Isaiah 6.16 we read 'Stand at the crossroads and look, ask for the ancient paths'.   When we look at the ancient path and study those who have travelled before, we see where they took hold of their opportunities and also where they struggled and fell. Their experiences warn us against making the same mistakes. We learn what hindered them from moving on and what encouraged them to get up again.   As we study them, we find that life is a pilgrimage.   Martin Wallace says that 'pilgrimage is a sacrament, an

22

outward sign of an inner spiritual grace.' He goes on to say that our life is a pilgrimage with God and into the heart of God.

David Adam also speaks of life as a journey: 'Sometimes the way is level and easy going and without hindrance – other times we find our way blocked and we can do nothing about it but wait.'

There is a great difference between being a pilgrim on a pilgrimage and those who travel just to look at the sights. The sights are good and we benefit from seeing how wonderful this world is, with its many cultures and magnificent achievements. It is wonderful to see the variety of colours, to smell the different aromas, and to hear the different tongues and accents. However, just to be a spectator means that you can easily miss the Presence or miss hearing the VOICE of the One who is present in every living thing all around us, all the time.

Goodness and Beauty

The longing on the journey is to enter deeper into the heart of God. In Genesis 1, after everything God had made, He said 'It is good'. He was so proud of what He had made, and rightly so, but He had no one to show it off to. Then He made man, and when He looked at man, He said 'It is very good'. I really think He said, 'Wow – that's real good!'

I often say to the young girls in Citylife when they think they look awful or are having a bad hair day, 'You look beautiful.' He who is beauty Himself cannot make anything or anyone who is not beautiful. But not one of these girls can accept the truth of that statement.

One Sunday afternoon when the house was full of young people, I said to one young girl, 'You look really lovely'.   She looked at me in astonishment and ran from the kitchen to the sitting room and said, 'Helene has just told me I look ugly.' You can imagine how bewildered I was.   I said to her 'Why did you say I thought you looked ugly when I said I thought you look lovely?' I will never forget her answer.   'Well', she said in her broad Scottish accent, 'You haven't said that before, so it means all the other days you thought I looked ugly'.

When God looked at His children He was like a proud Father as He said 'It's very good'. And that is what I want to know and experience, this goodness of God.   He made everything for us to enjoy. Not to appreciate it would be such a waste.

Since God is good and God is love, everything He made was out of love, whether we know it or not. For our life to be lived fully it must be a life of adventure. Jesus Himself did not lead a boring life, nor are we expected to, because when we are joined to the Lord we are one in spirit with Him. Where He goes we go: to walk on the water, to feed the poor, to quell the storm. We can even enjoy a meal with him.

On one occasion I took a group of young people and leaders from the ministry to the church in Toronto to let them experience something more of God. We had a great time. For many from the council estates, it was the first time on a plane, the first time eating in restaurants.   Before we went on this particular trip I realised how important it would be for the young people to eat together. I invited them round to my home for the first time and I discovered that some of them would not eat in front of me. After they became comfortable in my home they would eventually eat a bag of crisps. After another period of time I eventually managed to get them to eat a meal around the table. Many of the houses they live in have been built in such a way that there is no room for a dining table and so everybody eats with a plate on their lap. To eat in a restaurant meant that I had to wean them gently and gradually by first of all eating in front of someone and then eat together as a group. We did it!

In Toronto Airport Christian Fellowship a little boy went with the leading Pastor, John Arnott to pray for people. As the young boy put out his hand to bless a tall man who was waiting for prayer, the power of God came on the man and he fell to the floor. The little boy looked at his hand and said, 'Wow'. May we never lose the wonder and awe of a childlike life lived for Jesus.

Tourists or Pilgrims

We can journey and travel with no lasting effect - just photos in our album, or ancient memories. God wants to show us many things and talk to us about the intricate details of even a tiny cobweb, where each thread is so intricately woven together that the patterns it has is so incredible. A cobweb! What else can our eyes see that we have right before us and yet never really see? As our eyes are opened, we have cause to ponder even more on 'Who' made this wonderful world.

I remember being on an African Safari in Zimbabwe. One evening the group of us who had travelled together from Scotland were having a "sun-downer" on a boat on Lake Kariba. (A "sun-downer" is the custom of having a drink as you watch the sun set.)

We were not far from the shore of the lake when a herd of elephants passed by trumpeting their evening song. The sky was filled with a great big orange, yellow and red ball. It seemed for a short while that for me everything stopped. There was a song, or a harmony, in that moment in creation and the word from Job came to mind, 'My ears had heard of You, but now my eyes have seen You.' (42:5) I saw Him in the loveliness of that moment. As the beauty of that scene before me touched my heart, tears ran down my face. 'What's wrong?" asked my husband, quite concerned. 'Nothing, absolutely nothing! It's just so beautiful.' How good God is that He gave me this to enjoy, for my pleasure.

I realised that God is extravagantly good and that He cannot stop giving to His children, if we have eyes to see it and a heart to receive it. Sometimes I find myself crying with joy at His extravagant giving. It is as though He cannot stop giving, again and again. I am like a tiny daisy that He made so perfectly. God is not like my little seven-year old friend who was so bored with the journey of life. He so loved making the daisy that He made another and another and another. I think He simply enjoyed making them.

I think God had incredible fun as He and Adam named the animals. Where did Adam get the word 'hippopotamus'? As Adam said, 'This one is a hippopotamus,' I can imagine God saying, 'What? Where did Adam get that word? But okay. If that is what you want to call it – go ahead.'

That day in Zimbabwe I was no longer a tourist. I was a pilgrim, and I did not have to seek far to find Him because He is in every beautiful thing. Even in

Scotland on wet rainy days we can find His beauty in the rainbow or feel the rain wash our faces, making us feel clean and alive as though He is kissing us with His tears of joy.

God wants us to respond willingly to his invitation to 'Come.' Perhaps we know where we have come from as we begin this journey with Him, but we have no idea where we are going.

We are called to travel light on our journey and get rid of any excess baggage we carry. This is my story of how God helped me to begin to discard my own personal baggage that had become so part of me that I did not know it was there until I realised how heavy it was.

We often hesitate, stop or even go back on our journeying in the mistaken idea that God does not really want to hear our childlike talk about our desires. How silly are we? He gave us those desires in the first place. His desire is to bring wholeness to our brokenness. He gave His love to us, through His Son Jesus Christ. He was broken for us, so that we might begin to be healed and see the fulfilment of those desires.

As I continue on this journey, I am not sure what I will find after all these years because I have not stopped journeying, I have stopped crying out like the children, 'Are we nearly there yet?. It is actually quite freeing to know that we haven't made it.

The Pathway beneath the Journey

The one longing in my heart is that, even if I fall and life gets weary, I get up again and keep on going, because I want to know Him more and to finish the race well. I don't believe that God is as interested as we think in the things that cause us to fall. However, He is interested in our freedom. That is why He came - to bring us into the glorious freedom of the children of God. Anything that ties us up and causes us to fall does not bring us into the freedom that He came to give us. But what do we do? We focus on our sin and we become like the thing we focus on. The more we focus on our sin the more it traps us. The more we focus on the glorious freedom that He came to give us, the more free we will become. In the words of James Jordan: 'Don't' tell people what they have to do or what they have to become. Tell them who God is and what God does.'

'When you make a journey you uncover a pathway.'

It is essential to discover this pathway in a rootless culture, where nothing is solid beneath our feet. We desperately need stability, firm ground beneath our feet. We need to understand how to interpret the signposts and go in the right direction.

For me on this journey today, the signposts point me to a deeper journey, leading me into the interior of my own heart and the heart of the One who fills everything. New things wait to be discovered on our journey, a fresh awareness of the ever-present One who accompanies us every step of the way. The God of the whole universe, the Father of all fathers walks with us every moment of every day. We are never left alone fumbling around in the dark.

'Father, ever present God, awaken our spirit and our eyes to see You in the everyday situations and places we find ourselves. Tune us to Your VOICE so that we can hear your whisper - or even hear Your loud shout - saying, "This is the way, walk in it." Show us in a new way the wonder of a simple thing like a cobweb so that we can ponder the One who made it. Thank You, Father.'

Reflection

How do you feel as you realise that there is no arrival point in God? Relief and hope that there is still more to find out about this God who is mystery? Or do you feel angry because you thought you had made it, and crossed the finishing line?

How aware are you of the ever-present God as you go about your daily life? Do you take time to marvel at the "cobweb"?

CHAPTER THREE
MY TUMMY'S SORE

Sore Hearts - afraid to Dream

Have you ever wondered why children on a Monday morning often have a sore tummy? Generally, it is not that they are sick. When you probe more deeply, you find that someone at school has bullied them, that the teacher gave them a row, or that they didn't understand the lesson. It is not the tummy that is sore, but their heart is sore with pain and fear.

All of us have a dream inside us, but often our hearts are so sore that we are afraid to pursue our dreams. We feel we do not deserve them, or fear that we will never be able to achieve them. Some of us don't even recognise that we have a dream. Some years ago I asked a group of young people, 'What is the dream that you have in your heart? What would you like to be or do when you are older?' Many would shrug their shoulders, as if I was asking a very strange question, and say in a loud voice, 'I don't know. I dinnae ken.'

However, recently we have been asking the young people, 'What dream do you have for your life?' I was amazed when some of them came out and told us at Kid's church, 'I want to be a poet. I want to be a business manager and run my own company. I want to be a hairdresser'. How fantastic is that? I believe that there is a change going on in the children's hearts. I also believe that there is a slight change or shift in the spiritual climate. We still have a long way to go, but the harshness and hardness of hearts ten years ago seems to be slightly softening and melting.

People who do not work with inner city young people may not notice this, but I do. It seems as though God is doing something. God is at work in the present moment of every day, not afar off waiting and watching. His call is to be involved today in what He is doing, especially in this time of financial crisis. God has always promised to look after the poor, the widow and the orphan. Perhaps He is shaking the foundations of independent spirit.

By learning to listen to our hearts more and more, they will reveal to us what our treasure is. God placed this treasure within us at the beginning of time.

Living Outside In

There are many sore hearts around, but we are very good at covering it up. We live busy lives, religious lives, and even very moral lives, but avoid looking at our sore hearts.

My personality is such that I don't often take enough time to be still in order to hear my heart speak. When I ask myself why, it is possibly because I will have to suffer if I look inside. I do not like pain. Do any of us? Maybe the fear of suffering is worse than the pain itself. Below the pain there is a sense of desolation. We forget that God is deeper than our desolation.

However, it is important to embrace the desolation and not run from it. If we run away from it with hyper religious activity or the busyness of life, we will not face what is within us, and if we don't face what is within us, the emptiness and the loneliness, we will never find the God, who, by His Spirit, is deeper still.

My story is the beginning of healing at the levels or in compartments of our hearts that prevent us from falling in love fully with God and letting His love go deep into us. Why do we pretend and hide things? He knows all about us anyway. He has all understanding and understands us totally. He loves us just as we are, and yet we try to sort ourselves out before we come to Him because we feel He will not accept us just as we are.

The Way of the Heart

James Jordan of Fatherheart Ministries says on his website that 'God is calling us back to the ancient paths. A way of experiencing God that is discovered only through the heart.' The mind is very important, but there is greater depth to be found through experiencing God in our heart. Sometimes things are going on in our hearts that we cannot put into words. Then someone shares something and it brings a clarity to what is going on in our own heart. Our spirit leads and says, 'Yes, Yes, Yes'. 'What the mind cannot grasp, the heart can often hold.'

'Guard your heart with all diligence for out of it flow the issues of life.' (Proverbs 4:23) When trouble comes to our life and we hit "the wall", what is in our hearts comes to the surface, not what is in our mind. Who we are, and the way we experience life, is determined by who we are in our hearts. Jesus said, 'Out of the heart the mouth speaks.' Have we ever found that our mouth says things we did not want it to say? Sometimes we are quick to apologise and say, 'That wasn't me!' But we have to face is that it is us. The real motives in our hearts do come out of our mouths.

We can learn how to control what we say to give a good impression of how we want people to think of us. Unfortunately, a lot of Christian teaching is about making the right decisions and do doing the right things so that we look like the right kind of Christian. The problem is that there is a never-ending list of things that we have to do right. Sadly, we never know if we have made it. Meanwhile, our hearts remain unchanged.

However, in times of stress or hardships what is really in our hearts will come out. When you kick over the bucket, you find out what is really in it, be it sweet smelling or stale!

God wants to change our hearts so that it becomes instinctive to do His will because it flows from our heart. We are called to live our lives from our hearts. God is a God of the heart. Do we really believe that God just made a cold decision to love us? Or, is it because His heart is so full of love He cannot stop loving us.

'God does not look on outward appearances He looks on the heart.' (1 Samuel 16:7) We can do all the right outward things, but have no passion in our heart towards Him and God is not impressed one little bit. If our actions do not stem from the love that is in our hearts, they mean absolutely nothing.

The older brother in the story of the Prodigal son was like that. He did everything right and worked really hard, but the wayward younger son realised he had mucked it up. However he knew he was a son of the father even although he was rebellious. On his return home he came back with a broken and contrite heart. 'I'm sorry I have done everything wrong'. He acknowledged his mistakes, but the older brother was outside looking on at the party which the father was throwing for the return of his lost son. He was muttering to himself, 'How come I never get a party? I have worked for my father all these years.' The older brother did not realise that the father wanted to give him everything he had, but he had never asked. The father said, 'All that I have is yours'. Our heavenly Father says to us, 'All that I have is yours.' All we need is the heart of a child to receive His love and begin to walk in it.

We are all like the children when issues start to surface in the core of our being. Like them, we say, 'I have a sore tummy' – a sore heart in need of God's healing.

A Rucksack of Questions

Just as the children carried their picnic bags on the journey to the park, so we all carry a rucksack, as set off on our journey through life – a rucksack with a hundred and one questions. On journey we begin to find answers to the questions. Let me share with you some of the questions which troubled me – deep questions of the heart.

Question 1: 'Where are you, God?'

Maybe that is the wrong question. Maybe the question should be, 'Where aren't You?'

Deep in the heart of this universe is the very heart of God Himself. If we take time to look we can see evidence of His Presence absolutely everywhere. The wind reminds us of the Spirit and breath of God. The sun reminds us of the son of righteousness who rises with healing in his wings. 'Father open our eyes that we might see you'.

I have heard of two people recently who cried out to Jesus from deep within their hearts. It was not just an intellectual desire, it came as a deep yearning, 'Lord, I just want to see You. I just want to see your face'. In both cases, instantly the face of Jesus appeared to these two men. The two men lived at opposite sides of the world and yet their longing was the same and Jesus answered both their cries instantly.

They came to a deep realisation of the Lord who said, 'Lo, I am with you always, even unto the end of the age.' He is not a distant far off Lord who has left this world and will come back one day, but He is with us every moment of every day. That is what I need; an ever present God who is with me when I walk up and down the streets of the city.

Question 2: 'Will you let me suffer if I follow You?'

Maybe it is not the suffering we are fear, but the fear of suffering. Much of our time and energy is used in avoiding suffering instead of embracing it. If we are called to be a manifestation of Jesus who suffered, why do we think that we will be spared? I believe that there is a depth in God that we find only if we embrace the things that are in our lives rather than fighting against them.

One day when walking along the beach I found a cry rising from my own heart, 'I just want to know You. I don't want anything else. I just want to know You'. I did not make a mental decision that I wanted to know Him it just came bubbling out of the core of my being.

This cry comes from Paul himself. 'I want to know Christ, and the power of His resurrection and the fellowship of sharing in His sufferings.' (Phil 3:10) To really know Christ is to embrace suffering in whatever form. Some of the great mystics went through incredible suffering, but throughout their trials they found God in a way that many of us never do. We have the idea that God would never let us feel pain at that level. But I do not find any evidence of that in the Bible. Sometimes we feel that if pain or trouble comes to our life, we have done something wrong. Our understanding of God is so mixed up we believe He is out to punish us.

And yet David's psalms are full of his cries, 'Where are you God? 'How long will you forsake me?' These are the real cries of David who was known as a man after God's heart.

Question 3: 'Why do I feel abandoned, when I know you will never leave me?'

One of the children in our Kids Church has a fantastic ability to remember memory verses from the bible. When he was about ten years of age I asked him which verse meant the most to him. He quoted Joshua 1.5, 'I will never leave you nor forsake you'. Many of the young people remember this verse. I began to wonder why this one was so important to them. I believe that in the deep part of many of us there is an abandoned cry of loneliness that only be comforted by the revelation of words of the Father saying 'I will never leave you.'

Question 4: 'Why do I feel I have no place of belonging even within the church?

This is a key question. The truth of the matter is that we can do all the right things for God within the Church and be on every governing body within it. We can do the evangelism, teach in the Sunday School, feed the poor and a hundred and one other things, and still not feel you have a place because we become so busy doing things to get brownie points from God that we don't deal with the orphan issues that are deep within each one of us.

We will look at the orphan issues later. My coming home to the Father arose out of a measure of healing in this area.

Question 5: 'When I find You (or You find me!) why do I sometimes lose the sense of Your Presence?'

In Song of Songs the lover comes knocking on the door of the beloved, but by the time she answers it, he has run away. I believe that sometimes God withdraws Himself, not so that He cannot be found, but so that we will seek after Him.

Children playing with their Dad at 'hide and seek' often find their Dad hiding behind the couch with his feet sticking out. He wants to be found and he helps his child find him. I think God is like that.

Nowadays, being a little older and wiser, I get a kind of excitement when I cannot feel His Presence because I know that He is just around the corner. I experience something new about Him and have a fresh encounter that thrills my soul.

Question 6: 'What do I need to let go of?'

'Our fists are clenched and we are unable to stretch out open hands to receive the new thing, or person or insight God yearns to give us.'

We are all afraid of letting go, but if we hold on to what is familiar all the time then we cannot embrace the new experiences that God wants to give us.

In order to respond with our heart, there are issues within us, like the questions in our backpack, that block us. The chapters that follow address some of the factors that stopped me from fully abandoning myself to God fully, and spell out the restoration that He brought to bring me into freedom.

The key to Christian maturity is based on one simple thing: our ability to receive love. That makes it so much easier. The key to receiving love is becoming a little child who needs to be loved. God restores our souls as He imparts His love to us because our greatest need is that God will be a Father to us. He said, 'I will be a Father to you'. This not about knowing all the biblical references about God being a Father, but letting Him be a Father to us. We may know that 'God is love', but it is another thing to know that He is loving us right now. Right this moment as you read these words, God is loving you right now.

The only thing that will make any difference to our lives is that we allow His love to be poured into our hearts. The Father was the only source for Jesus' life. He is the only source for our life. Jesus said, 'I am the way, the truth and the life, no one comes to the Father but by Me'. That is why Jesus came. It is so simple. He came to reveal the Father. The gospel is about a Father who lost His children and who wants them back so much that He sent His Son to bring us home.

Jesus is the door. I used to believe He was the door we had to go through to get to heaven, but James Jordan says, 'It is the door for the Father to get to us.' That is wonderful! He comes to us – to meet us heart to heart.

REFLECTIONS

Look at the questions above and see how they relate to your life.

Question 1: Where are you God?

Have you ever asked that question? If so what were the circumstances surrounding it?

Can you think of any evidence that you felt God's Presence was with you?

Question 2: Will You let me suffer if I follow You?

Look at the reason why you asked that question. For my own life, I did not have a grasp of His goodness and His protection. I had a false idea of what God was like. What is your God like?

Question 3: Why do I feel abandoned when I know you will never leave me?

Have you ever felt totally alone? If so what were the circumstances surrounding that experience? Is this something you experience all the time?

Question 4: 'Why do I feel I have no place of belonging even within the church?

We are never expected to live life in isolation, but to be part of a Church family, which means opening up to one or two trusted people. If we live a life of privacy, then no one gets to know who we really are.

Question 5:'When I find You (or You find me!) why do I sometimes lose the sense of Your Presence?'

Do you have someone who can be a listening ear for you in these times? If not, I encourage you to find someone that you can trust. Celtic Christianity calls this 'soul friendship.'

Question 6: What do I need to let go of?

In order to move into the new thing that God wants to give us, we often have to release something before we can embrace the new beginning. Are you holding on to something that has your identity tied up in it?

For me I gave up Youth Work for a short time because I did not want my value and worth to be found in what I did.

CHAPTER FOUR
SAY MY NAME

Lost in the Crowd

Have you ever been part of a large crowd and felt totally lost. It could be amongst the throng at a football match, at a disco or amongst the Saturday shoppers at the Mall. Or is it just me that feels like a dot on the landscape sometimes?

That is how I felt attending a Conference at Toronto Airport Christian Fellowship in the 1990s where people were people gathered for worship and to hear the Word of God. You had to queue for an hour to get a seat near the front, just hoping that the speaker would notice you and that he or she might have a word from God for you. How could God give a word to someone who felt invisible? He could not see you! I felt totally unseen amongst the 5,000 people who were attending. All the important people were in the reserved seats at the front, or on the platform, but I was lost in the middle of a row, in the middle of the auditorium.

Perhaps that is why when the Holy Spirit starts to move with genuine manifestations showing His presence and His power through our physical bodies, it sometimes brings a sense of lostness to those who do not experience anything. If He doesn't touch us, and I we can feel left out.

However, some people seem to have more needs, and need to be noticed more than others and they somehow have exaggerated manifestations. Their body movements imply, 'Look I can jerk more than you. I can laugh louder than you. I can fall down more easily than you.' Most of this stems from the one basic need in all our lives, 'Will someone please notice me?'

I remember when this incredible, genuine move of God was at its height, I was sitting thinking over what the speaker had been talking about and noticed a young woman on the floor. Her look was one of, 'Would someone please notice me?' We were encouraged at that point to pray for someone close by so I went over and gently affirmed that God saw her and knew that she was there. Instantly she lay at peace with a smile on her face. It doesn't take much to notice a person and affirm her. A few words are all it takes.

I love the work of the Holy Spirit and often would get so drunk in the Spirit I had to be helped home. Sometimes His work in my life during those fun days made me realise that we were just a lot of children enjoying playing in the river of His love that was flowing during those years. None of us really knew how to handle it.

That is why I honour John and Carol Arnott for pastoring this incredible move of God and affirming it as the Father's blessing. They made everyone feel welcome. There were no judgements in them when things happened that were the manifestations of man, because they recognised what was real and genuine as well as the deep desires of people to be noticed. All they longed for was that the Father would make Himself real to them.

I believe this deep longing to be noticed is true for all of us at some time in our lives, if not for some of us all the time. We just want someone to notice us. Often we feel alone, and left out, having the strong feeling that we don't belong, even feeling we don't have a place in the Body of Christ, the Church. On the other hand, there are some who feel that they alone have the ear of God and view themselves as the ones on the inside. From that viewpoint they feel that their way alone is right. When people feel like that they form their own denomination or their own group, or their own club. It is really important to admit the feelings of isolation and loneliness that pervades all of us from time to time and face the reality that none of us has all truth. Only Christ Himself can say that.

Say my Name

During the course of that particular Conference, a woman called Judith McNutt spoke at one of the seminars. I have no recollection of her topic, but a few words resonated in my heart, 'Have you ever heard God call your name?' 'Know my name,' I said to myself, 'No. I don't think He even knows that I exist, or that I am even here.' And yet I could preach on the verse, 'I will never leave you nor forsake you', or, 'I have called you by name, you are mine'. It is a funny thing that we can give talks on subjects that are not even a reality in our own life. We can have a theological understanding, but no heart revelation. All that this means for us is an echoing sound which has no reality or substance in our lives.

I responded to her question by saying to myself, 'No, God, I have never heard you say my name, but I would like to ask you to say my name and that you say it in a way I will understand'. I did not take a long time to make this request. There were no choirs singing for me, or an audible voice of God asking me to respond. I said this with a matter-of-fact statement. It had no emotion. It was said without faith. It was just a simple request like a child asking for a sweet, 'Father, would you give me a sweet? Father, would you say my name?'

I am not sure of the date of that Conference, but over the months following I kept hearing a refrain from a popular song that was being sung by some of the young people in Citylife, 'Say my name, say my name, say my name'. So I would sing it to God too, just in case He had forgotten I had asked Him to say my name. This phrase 'say my name' began for me to have a rhythm to it, a kind of melody and a harmony that began to take root in my heart. 'Say my name, say my name, say my name'.

During the later months of the year 2000 I was visited by a representative of ChildLine, which is an organisation that helps young people in crisis in the United Kingdom. Once a year there is an award given to someone whose service is to young people. Even to be considered for this award you have to be nominated by a child. I did not know it at the time, but two boys in our Kids Church, Stuart and Stephen Kenny had put my name forward for the nomination for the B.T. ChildLine Award for the year 2000. They were about 7 and 11 years old at that time. One day they had been sitting watching the television when the children's programme Newsround came on and the host of the show was saying, 'Do you know someone who has done a lot in the community and a lot for children. And if you do, would you like to do something about it?' Their mother told me that they discussed it together and they said, 'Why don't we nominate Helene because she feeds the people and runs buses for children to go to Kid's Church'. So they filled in the application form and sent it off.

Many names are put forward for this award and after the Committee had gone through the applications that children had sent in, they make a decision to invite four finalists they have chosen, as possible candidates for the Award.   These four finalists were invited to attend the Ceremony in London and each of the finalists was given permission to take a guest with them. As one of the four finalists, I took one of my granddaughters, Hannah, to accompany me for two reasons: one reason was that the award was for serving young people and it seemed appropriate to take someone young (she was nine years old at the time); however, the second reason I invited her to join me was that I wanted her to know how special she was. Although I worked alongside many young people, she was very important to me. She accompanied me, with an air of excitement, along with the two boys who had nominated me.

These awards are presented by the Duchess of Kent and Esther Rantzen, the President of ChildLine.   To quote Esther Rantzen, 'Children are the best judges of the adults who work to increase their happiness and protect them from pain.'   I think that children are very much on the heart of our Father, but sometimes society, and even the Church, regard them as of no value.   Sometimes there is the feeling that those who work with the young have a lesser role than those who teach the adults, because adults are more important. However, Jesus Himself considered children of high value and even said, 'Unless you become like a child you cannot even enter the Kingdom of God'.   A heart attitude that is childlike shows our dependency on people and admits our need of God as a Father.

The ceremony was held in the centre of London in a very up-market hotel, whose name I have forgotten. At most of these events they give the names of the runners up first and then the name of the finalist. After the names of the three runners up had been given, Esther Rantzen put on her white sash and said, 'The winner of this year's ChildLine Award is Helene King'.

I was overcome with emotion. Not because I had won the Award, which was fantastic, but, as I got up to receive it, God spoke to me and said, 'You wanted me to say your name – well, because I am so proud of you, I'm saying it publicly'. This was said as the T.V. cameras rolled and the newspaper cameras flashed. I cannot begin to tell you what that meant for me. Winning the Award was incredible, but what made the difference and a major turning point in my life was the fact that God knows my name, and that, if He knows my name, He knows everything about me.

It has become my life's passion to be used to bring healing to the hearts of people, especially the young, so that they too can know the Father knows their name. When you know that your Father, who just happens to be Almighty God knows your name then there is no way that you can feel invisible again.

The prize for the Award was £5,000, which could be given to any charity of your choice. It is interesting to note here that the timing of God is perfect because at that precise moment, Citylife Ministries was being set up as a charity and one of its main aims was to help young people in the inner city to have a VOICE and not just to have a VOICE, but to be heard.   There are no prizes for guessing which the charity of my choice was.   What a wonderful way to start a ministry.   It was truly the blessing and goodness of God.

Will you ride with me?

Six years later, I had a dream. I had the same dream twice in the same night which, I have learnt since, is very significant. In my dream, I saw a White Horse. This Horse was moving with such speed that it seemed stationary, if that makes sense.   This White Horse was not riding on the ground, but in the sky. The White Horse came close and stopped right in front of me.   What was even more amazing to me, even in my dream, is that when it spoke it addressed me by name.   This White Horse knew my name, which of course meant a lot to me.   I wonder now on looking back as I write this, if I needed a bit of encouragement at that time.

He asked me a question. I have discovered that when God speaks, He uses very few words.   What He said to me was this, 'Helene, will you ride with Me?'   As I looked at this White Horse, I saw that He had the kindest eyes I have ever seen.   As He asked this question and waited for my reply I thought that, like Jesus, He invites. He issued me with an invitation. 'Helene, will you ride with Me?'   I looked past His face and saw that His back was bare.   There was no saddle on His back, no reins with which to hold on to – nothing.   The enormity of the question He asked made me think before I answered.   This was no little question.   If I got on His back, there was nothing with which I could guide Him.   This meant that He would be in charge. As He rode I would feel the wind of the Spirit on me, but I would not know where He would lead me, or where He would take me. I thought about this question because if I said 'Yes' I would have no right to my own life anymore. I would have to go where He went. But what else could I say but 'Yes'.

It may seem strange, but to me this White Horse was symbolic of the Holy Spirit. In Celtic spirituality, the Wild Goose represented the Holy Spirit. When the White Horse came across to me, He had that same wildness, but he was also incredibly gentle.

I believe that He is extending to all who hear it an invitation to come and ride with Him and go wherever He goes. There is a great need to abandon ourselves to hear the ONE VOICE that speaks to us words of love and affirmation. A VOICE that calls us into a wild adventure that leads us to travel the seas, to climb the mountains, to fly on the wings of the wind. This VOICE leads us to a Person. To experience this Person we need to abandon ourselves fully to Him. We begin to move towards the place where we give up everything, every moment of our daily life. In fact it changes the whole course of our life.

The Voice calls

This VOICE spoke to multitudes by the Sea of Galilee. This VOICE once spoke a sermon on the mount. This VOICE speaks today telling us not to worry. This VOICE gives us an awareness of the life that we are living, giving us an invitation to follow Him, offering us a life to be lived.

When we become aware of this VOICE in the present moment of everyday living, we find that we have a choice to make to follow Him or reject Him. This VOICE speaks to us of higher things, of things that are much more important. This VOICE tells us that He clothes the grass of the field which is here for a brief moment and then gone forever, so why should we worry about what to wear or what to eat when He has promised always to provide and take care of us if we just listen and obey this VOICE.

The VOICE of our own reasoning must be left behind and abandoned in order to listen to the VOICE that speaks to us in a still gentle whisper. To listen to this VOICE within it is necessary to leave behind the world's noise and bustle and find a place of quiet where things are much more simple and not so complicated and noisy.

This VOICE calls us to forget the past and to concentrate on the present moment and to leave the future in the hands of the ONE whose VOICE is within.

When Jesus was walking along the streets of the towns in Judea He was constantly bumping into fishermen, tax collectors and prostitutes. Often He stopped and said to them, 'Follow Me'. Astonishingly these people abandoned their careers, their families, their homes, in fact everything to follow Jesus. All because He gave a simple invitation, 'Follow Me'.

Why? Why would these men and women give up everything that was familiar to them to follow Jesus into what they didn't know? Perhaps it was because somehow they knew that life with Jesus was the life they had been seeking all their lives. Which goes beyond the confines of safety and caution. They knew in their spirits that life's greatest adventure was waiting, just beyond what was familiar and safe to them.

I believe that when Jesus called these simple people to follow Him He was saying by His invitation that He saw great potential in them. He was saying to come and take on the yoke that He carried, the rabbi's yoke. By asking them to do this He was in reality saying to them, 'You can be like Me'. How awesome is that? 'You can be like Me'.

When people became their rabbi's disciple and followed him they were, by their decision, agreeing with that rabbi's teaching and his ways of interpretation of the Scripture. When Matthew, and the others that Jesus chose left their jobs with their father's business, they were saying by their very actions 'You believe in us, and we want to come under your yoke and become like You.' So many in the Christian Church want to be like Jesus and believe that to become like Jesus we copy Him in what He does. But that is not becoming like Him. To become like Him means that our hearts and spirits become so connected with His that we gradually become more and more like Him.

Jesus said, 'Whoever loses His life for My sake will find it.' In other words, whoever abandons his life will live life to the full.

Why don't we all make a decision to really go for it? Why don't we taste the new wine of the kingdom that is flowing in our time? Why don't we drink the living water instead of drinking from the cracked broken cisterns that Jeremiah spoke about?

The life of adventure that He is inviting us to join is a life that throws caution to the wind, where danger and risk await. Jesus is really saying, 'Abandon yourself to the ONE VOICE who will never abandon you'. If we were all really honest with ourselves most of us have lost touch with the childlike excitement of abandonment. We believe in Jesus. We love the idea of Jesus. We try to do what we believe He wants us to do, but to abandon everything? We so want to be like Him – but that is what He was like. To abandon our job, our security, our nice home or whatever we have sounds crazy. Abandonment is unpredictable.

All we need to ride the White Horse is a sense of wonder and childlike trust that takes His Presence seriously. Hearing His VOICE becomes easier as we bend our ear to His and sense the rhythm of the dance as we are being called to move and flow with Him. There is nothing static in the journey of walking with our Lord.

Reflection

1. Do you feel that God doesn't know your name? Are there any particular circumstances or events that you can recall when you felt lost?

If you don't know that God knows your name, ask Him to say it. He will not answer your prayer in the way He answered mine because He treats everyone of us differently.

2. Jesus Christ, the Son of God, is extending an invitation to you right now: Will you ride with me? His hand is outstretched towards you.

Stand up and stretch out your hand as a gesture that you are willing to respond to His invitation. Take the first tentative steps that a baby takes when learning to walk. If you fall, and you will, you will find that He is at your side, lifting you up.

CHAPTER FIVE
ALL BY MYSELF

Alone and Abandoned

One of the young men in Citylife called Matthew has struggled most of his life with a real sense of isolation and loneliness. He has been coming to Citylife for a couple of years and he often goes about singing a song entitled 'All By Myself'. It is quite a catchy song by Celine Dion, but I began to realize one day when I was speaking at Church that we can often have an orphan spirit which manifests itself by having no place of belonging. Like Matthew we can be part of a group but still feel as if we are 'All By Myself'. If we don't feel we have a place of belonging in our Father's House, the Church, we often find also that we don't feel we have a place in our Father's world. We can live a life all on our own even surrounded by many people. That was true for me.

I believe that there is an unprecedented cry rising from the earth from the hearts of people. This is the cry of the Fatherless. I have heard this cry as part of a large meeting in Toronto, at a time when many people were being touched by the Holy Spirit. There was a lot of laughter and outbreaks of joy, but I was lying on the carpet just resting in God's presence when I heard the crying of hundreds of people. I sat up and looked around but no one was crying. It was not until some years later that I realised that the cry I heard in my spirit was the cry of the fatherless. More than any other generation gone before us has there been such a depth of people who feel abandoned, rejected and orphaned.

The only thing that takes away this orphan spirit is love, the love of our heavenly Father being poured into our spirit. In John 14 as Jesus is about to leave his disciples he speaks these incredible words, 'I will not leave you as orphans'. When someone is about to leave, you want to hang on to his last words. Jesus was speaking to his trusted companions and disciples that he had poured his life into these last words, 'I will not leave you as orphans'. They were not physical orphans - James and John were brothers who had a job in their father Zebedee's business, fishing with him every day – but when he left, Jesus sent the Holy Spirit, known as the Paraclete, the one who is called "alongside', the Comforter so that they would not be alone.

If that is true, why do so many of us struggle like young Matthew in Citylife?

We can have a theological understanding of God as our Father and the Holy Spirit as the Comforter, but not know that reality in our lives. We have no experiential revelation that has touched us in the core of our being.

The truth of this became very real to me when I was attending a month long school entitled 'The Father heart of God' in Toronto. One speaker happened to ask in the course of his talk 'Have any of you ever felt abandoned?' I had left the room to get a drink of water and was walking back to my seat, minding my own business, just as Ed Piorik was saying these words. 'Have any of you ever felt abandoned?'

Without any process of reasoning, I burst into tears - not just a little cry. I was howling and I didn't understand why.   My father and mother hadn't divorced. I had not been put in a children's home. I had not been neglected in any way whatsoever.   I had not been passed to someone else. I just could not understand what was going on inside me. I was crying so much for the next period of time, that Julia and Graeme Mackel, who are on the Citylife Core Team and attended the School with me, said that they should call me 'Jeremiah, the weeping prophet', but, since I was female, they nicknamed me 'Jemima, the weeping prophetess'. It sounds funny and we began to laugh, but to me it was very painful. It was not until sometime later I began to understand what had been going on inside me as I looked back on my life.

Stories of Home

When I was about three years of age, the Second World War was raging so there was an incredible amount of fear gripping the hearts of people. During this period of time my father was in hospital. He had been out playing football when he tripped over a tuft of grass and broke his spine. He was in hospital for a very long time and we could only get to visit him once a week because the hospital was an hour away by bus outside the city.

We lived in a top flat in one of Edinburgh's old tenements in Marchmont, near the city centre, so when the sirens went off my mother had to take my younger sister and I down the stairs to the air raid shelter in the back garden. Since I was only young and the steps were very high for a tiny child, it was quite a struggle to get down. The noise, the fear, the panic all grabbed a little girl's heart.

Since my father, through no fault of his own, was in hospital for such a long time, we had very little money coming in. A spirit of poverty and abandonment began to take root in my heart and, as I grew older, I always lived with insufficiency. Even though I had enough, it never seemed to last. I lived on second hand clothes. Second hand comics and a small bag of sweets was all my weekly pocket money could buy. I still remember the occasional Saturday visits to the second hand shops in the Grassmarket. Living like this over the war years put within me, without realizing it, a mentality that said 'I would never have enough'. Not only that, but, on reflection, I felt that was all I was worth. I didn't deserve better. I didn't know why. I hadn't done anything wrong, but that is what I believed.

I always had a desire to help people. In the tenement stair next to ours, also on the top flat, there lived a family I came to know very well. The husband was a dentist, but his wife and daughter rarely went out. The daughter, although older than I, was badly deformed. Although I saw her deformities, I liked her and we got on well together. I would go for their shopping and often was given a plaster mould set of false teeth as payment! They were made of plaster of Paris they made good chalks! I was the only kid on the block who drew hopscotch lines on the pavement outside with a set of dentures. All the other kids had boxes of chalk. I know it's really funny, and I laugh as I think about it now, but you can imagine what the other kids said. I think that this developed more within me a sense of 'I'm not worth as much as the other kids'.

It wasn't until the year 2003 that the effect of those early years came to light as Ed Piorik said those words that opened the floodgates, 'Have any of you ever felt abandoned?'   Who we are today is who we have been.   The effect on a child who was abandoned at three years of age, when she becomes five or six or even sixty six, is still part of who she is unless our heavenly Father pours His love into the broken places and the empty place of abandonment.

When we feel abandoned by our earthly father, even though it is not his fault, we develop a sense of no one noticing us. Those formative years of my early life developed within me the heart of an orphan.

As we look briefly at what it means to live life as an orphan, we may see similar traits in our own lives.

The Orphan Spirit

An orphan has no name and although I had a name it is significant to note that I did not believe that anyone, including God, knew my name.   An orphan has no identity, has no real sense of who he is.   An orphan does not know what a family is because he grows up with other orphans and only gets what he fight for.   An orphan thinks differently from others, with a 'poverty mindset'.

The ways of this world are orphan ways.   The ways of this world is to fight for what we need and to place our security in what is in the bank. An orphan receives no gifts in life.

When I was in my early twenties, and before I was married, because of my love for children I used to take children out from an orphanage. One day I took a group of four boys to my parent's home to celebrate one of the children's birthdays. We had a small birthday cake and some sandwiches. I cut the cake into two halves and divided one of the halves into four for the boys to eat during the party. The rest of the cake was to be divided up so that each of the boys could take a party bag home. One of the boys wanted to take the half that had been laid aside. I said to him, 'Why not take a small slice now so that you can have a piece to take home?' I also arranged that when the games were played each one of the boys would win a bar of chocolate or a bag of sweets so that each would have something. They were encouraged to put it in their party bag ready to take back to the children's home.

This particular boy kept going over every few minutes to the table where the bags were. I told him, 'Don't worry. No one will take it from you. I am here to see that everything is given out fairly'. I will never forget his words, 'You don't understand. I might not get anything to eat tomorrow'. This boy lived life in a children's home and although he was fed on a regular basis the part of him that had not been healed believed that he could go hungry again. He was living as an orphan.

By the rules of this world, you get no presents at all. Everything you receive you earn - you have to work for what you get. Salvation can be difficult for people because they believe they have to earn it. Work and earn. That is the way it works.

An orphan has trouble being generous because he has worked hard for everything he gets and he wants to hold on to it. This mindset can also manifest itself within the Church. If a leader has received some anointing from God, he can be very jealous about giving it away because his core belief is that I might not receive any more.

To everything there is a beginning. The question we have to ask ourselves is, 'Where did the first orphan come from?' We read in Isaiah 14 that the great desire of Satan was to be like God. He wanted to ascend and take the throne from God Himself. God will not share His glory with anyone and so Satan was cast out of heaven taking a third of the angels with him, and he became the first spiritual orphan. His great desire is to get as many of us that he can to become like him.

I believe that heaven is full of the Father's presence. Satan did not want that and so it became impossible for him to live there. The atmosphere of heaven is the atmosphere of the Father and Satan did not want a Father. God is creator and God is healer, But these are what He does. Father is who He is.

An orphan spirit can be found within the Church as well as in the world, and it is found not just in the leadership. Christians may say that it is their zeal and prayers, or fasting and tithing that move the heart of God. But God responds to his children, not because of our efforts. The only way to replace our orphan ways is to introduce our heart to the Father Himself. His love being poured into our spirit takes away the isolation and abandonment.

One good test of knowing how much revelation we have received of the Father's love is to look at how much fear is in our lives.   Orphans experience many kinds of fear – fear of the future, fear of failure, fear of what people think of you, fear of authority, to name but a few. As the love of the Father becomes a greater reality in our lives, the fear slips away.   The bible says that perfect love takes away fear. Nothing else. Not trying to pretend it is not there, not trying to cast it out, not quoting scripture, not trying to become a victorious overcomer.   None of these things will get rid of fear, nothing but His wonderful love poured into the depths of our being.

Orphans or Sons and Daughters

Let us look briefly at the difference between an orphan and a son.   The truth is that we are all sons of God, but often our lives do not demonstrate the place of sonship.

The orphan spirit takes delight in accusing other people and exposing them.   But love covers all wrongs.   Love covers a multitude of sins. In Genesis chapter 3 we find that after Adam and Eve had sinned they found themselves exposed and naked. They went away and hid.   However, when the Father found them He clothed them in the skins of animals to take away their shame.   Love covers.   Love covers all wrongs. (Proverbs 10.12)

In Genesis 9 we read the story of Noah's drunkenness. When Ham, the father of Canaan, saw his father's nakedness, he ran outside the tent and began to expose his father Noah by telling his brothers about their father's sin. Often young people in Citylife love to come and tell me the latest gossip. 'Helene do you know what so and so has done?' They love to be the ones that know everything because it makes them feel part of the 'in crowd'. I can imagine that when Ham came out of the tent there would be a kind of furtiveness about him, an air of secrecy because he knows something his brothers didn't. I love what his brothers Shem and Japheth did, they took a blanket and walked backwards, without looking at their father, and they covered his nakedness. Love covers.

Orphans have a great longing to be the best achievers in all things, but a son is overwhelmed with thanks for all that his Father has given to him and done for him. Orphans want to be praised for everything they do, but a son just knows that he is accepted in the love of the Father not because of anything he has done. An orphan may have a great desire to be holy and do all the right things to have his Father's favour, but a son's only desire is to have intimacy and through that intimacy becomes holy. An orphan has a deep sense of emptiness and wants to have comfort above all else and to fill that emptiness he seeks for it in things to try and fill the void, but a son seeks times of solitude and quiet and rest in his Father's presence. An orphan does not allow the deepest part of him to be revealed, but a son is open-hearted and admits his struggles and his weaknesses.

If you have identified with any of the above orphan ways, I have incredible good news for you. An orphan is in desperate need for a father. Webster's dictionary says that 'a father is one who gives us significance'. A father gives us a sense of destiny and purpose – He is the one for whom we want to get out of bed in the morning.

A father would say to you, 'You have a place here. You have a place in my heart. You don't have to perform. You don't have to meet all the demands – you are loved for who you are'.

The only question we have to ask ourselves is, 'Can you be a little boy or girl who needs to be loved'. Only children need a Father. I say this again and again because this is so true. Only children need a Father.

Wanted! Spiritual Fathers and Mothers

I believe it is vitally important in this day and hour to raise up spiritual fathers and mothers because they impart blessing. Everything that has life receives life from its parents. Spiritual life imparts spiritual life. A father gives a name and an identity. You know who you are. A son draws from a spiritual father and draws fathering from him. A spiritual father is one who has a child-likeness and people can draw that from him.

The bible says that we have many teachers but few fathers. How true that is. You can get from any Christian bookshop, books or audio teachings on every subject or theme in the Bible. You can download sermons on the web. You can order teaching and worship songs and a million and one other things over the internet that give insight into spiritual things, but you cannot get a spiritual father or mother that way.

One of my concerns today is that there is much teaching on the Fatherheart of God and many people teach on becoming spiritual fathers and mothers in the Body of Christ. That is wonderful, but it is becoming the latest topic. However, you cannot give what you have not first received yourself. It often troubles me that so few leaders in the Church will go forward for ministry and admit that they need someone to pray for them. It seems that we are becoming what the bible talks about 'the wise and prudent', but God reveals these things to children.

Reflection

1. Do you identify with any of the orphan issues mentioned above?

The good news is that God wants to reveal Himself as a Father, but He is waiting for your invitation so that He can come to you and wrap His warm arms of love around you, like a warm blanket, giving security and a place of safety. The only safe place in this world is resting in the Father's arms.

2. Do you have someone that you consider to be a spiritual father or mother to you?

It may not be someone that you see regularly or it may be someone who when they speak you can draw life from them. They impart revelation to you. When you look into their eyes, you know that they know the Father.

A spiritual father or mother may not necessarily know about it. James Jordan does not know that I consider him my spiritual father, but I love to be occasionally where he is to drink from what he is saying. We don't listen to good preachers. We drink from them. Spiritual fathers and mothers are around if we have just eyes to see them.

"Father, come with your love and wrap your arms around our spirits and love us to life, the real life that you have promised to give to your sons and daughters. Help us to recognise our orphan ways. We call on you to reveal yourself to us deep in the core of our being so that we can truly live as sons and daughters of Almighty God living life with our Father. Amen"

CHAPTER SIX
YOU'LL NEVER WALK ALONE

A Divine Appointment

My journey from poverty to the beginning of living with sufficiency began in Toronto Airport Christian Fellowship (TACF). You must wonder why I went to TACF so many times. Andrew Murray, a great spiritual leader some years ago, said, 'If you are looking for someone, you need to go where he may be found'. I believed God was in TACF.

However I am aware that I could give the impression that I thought He was not anywhere else, and, of course, that is not true. God is present everywhere by His Spirit. God is in Scotland where I live, but the specific manifestation of His Presence was not here. Meanwhile, in Toronto the Presence of God was not only visible, but there were also so many testimonies of lives being changed and transformed by the Father's blessing that I wanted to experience this for myself.

While I was attending the same school that had such an impact on me in the dealing with the issue of abandonment, I came to experience His love for me in a way that helped me to come into a greater understanding of finding my Father in a fresh, and real way. James Jordan of Fatherheart Ministries based in New Zealand was one of the speakers at the school at an open evening meeting at the Church. I did not know this man. I had never heard of him until the year 2003, but I had a strong nudge that I must go and hear what he had to say. When you receive a nudge like that, you have a choice to go with the nudge or to push it aside. The feeling was so strong within me that I had to go and hear what he had to say, even though that meant cancelling going out with a group of friends that I had met at the school

I had a strong impression in my spirit that I had a divine appointment with God, so I went to the church meeting. James began his sermon with the verse from the apostle Paul to the Galatian Church chapter 3 'You are all sons of God'. These words, and in fact the whole of his sermon, had me just about jumping out of my seat. These words kept echoing in my heart, and in my mind, 'I am a son of God'. (There is no gender here in this statement by Paul) 'I am a son of God' How awesome is that! Then it dawned on me, 'If I am a son of God, then He really is my Father.' What a revelation! He was my real Father, the one I had been looking for all my life.

I've got it!

As I have said before, we can have a theological knowledge of God as our Father, but have no real experience of it. If He really is my Father then I was free from all the orphan ways that I had felt within me, such as not having a place of belonging because orphans don't belong anywhere, feeling isolated and alone, living with the core belief that no one knows your name, having little in material wealth because orphans don't have anything in the way of worldly goods. In time all the effects of this would begin to slip away and be replaced by the only One who can take away the feelings of being an orphan, the love of God as a Father.

As James was speaking, I began to realise that, if my Father is Almighty God, then whatever I needed in life He would supply.   When James said that God is calling us into the glorious freedom of the sons of God, I could hardly contain myself.   Like a child catching a ball being thrown. 'I've got it'. 'I've got it'.   I really had got it.   I understood it for the first time in my whole Christian life.

To explain why this experience was so real to me I need to take you back to about 1993. I was reading my bible one afternoon in my home, not expecting anything significant to happen, just obeying the daily discipline of trying to get to know God through His word, when I read these words from Titus 3.5   'He saved us, not because of righteous things we had done, but because of His mercy.' His word began to echo in my heart and in my mind.   I kept hearing Him say, 'I saved you not because of anything you have done'. He said. 'I've saved you because you are you, not because of any of your good works, but because of My mercy.'

Buying God's Favour

I had spent many years involved in Church activities. I was in charge of the youth, evangelism co-ordinator and a hundred and one other things, to the point that there was no fun or joy in it any more. It is as though I was trying to win 'Brownie points' with God. It is like the people who worshipped Baal. They believed that the bigger the gift, the bigger the return should be to the giver. The Baal worshippers eventually began to think that if they wanted a greater return for their harvest, the greater the gift should be given to the gods. Eventually they reached the stage where they began to cut themselves, as though the shedding of their blood would bring a greater return for their offering.

Sometimes I wonder if it is like that with us in the Church. We may say that all our sacrifices are for the One and Only God but I think that we truly believe that the greater our sacrifice - the more we do, the louder our prayers, the longer the fasting, the greater our giving - then the more the gods (whoever they are) will hear us. We carry this into Christianity. We have forgotten what God has said in Titus, 'I have saved you not because of righteous acts you have done but because of My mercy'. When we serve God like that our understanding of who God is and what He is like is totally wrong.

If God is love and God is our Father, then why would He want us to wear ourselves out in trying to please Him with more and more sacrifices. The only thing God is after is our heart. All He wants us to do is love Him and our service and our walk with Him begins to flow from our heart. We give to our Father because we can't hold back. We love because He first loved us. When we live a life of compulsive sacrificial giving, we are really conveying that we are afraid of Him. We are afraid that if we don't serve Him enough then He might cause, or allow bad things to happen. Some people might worry that, if they cheated on the speed limit while driving along the road in the car, then perhaps that is why they were made redundant from their job. If they kicked the cat or were rude to their neighbour perhaps that is why they developed cancer. When we step back away from these scenarios, we realise how silly and stupid we really are. This is not the God of the Bible, because the Bible speaks of a God who loves us and loves this world that He has created.

Amazing Grace!

I had become weary in well doing, but I was developing within me, at that time, the beginning of a great hunger for the Word of God. After He spoke to me from the book of Titus, I decided I would take time out to study the bible in more detail. I began to question to myself, 'What should I study'? During this period of time there was a lot of talk in the Christian Church about grace and I realized that those words from Titus 3.5 were really referring to the grace of God. Grace is the unmerited favour of God: there was nothing I could do that would make Him love me more, and there was nothing I had done that would make Him love me less. Why? Because God is the embodiment of love and He cannot do anything else but love.

I have begun to understand that love is a greater motivator to following Jesus Christ than anything else. I began to realise Jesus' words, 'I and my Father will come to you and we will make our home within you.' If, by the power of the Holy Spirit, the divine Trinity lives within me, then we can begin to have a homecoming, moving deeper into the very heart of who God is. We begin to lose our orphan ways and we can begin to love God. Why would we willingly want to sin when He gave up everything because of His love for us. Truly knowing how much He loves me causes me to want to love Him more and not hurt or offend the One who came to bring us into the glorious freedom of the sons of God.

Grace and Peace

I began another stage in my journey by going to the Christian bookshop to find material in order to begin my study on considering what grace really meant.

In many of the books in the New Testament written by Paul he introduces nearly every one of his letters to the churches with the words 'grace and peace'. Whether he wants to encourage the people or even rebuke them when they need it, he always starts with these words, 'Grace and peace to you.' Grace means to bless someone with no expectation of any return. Would it not be wonderful if we began to use these words when we meet one another? What would it be like if we began to wish one another grace without expecting anything in return? What would it be like if we truly knew that 'we will never walk alone' and we could wish grace and peace even for our enemies. I need to be reminded of the grace of God regularly for myself.

Paul understood grace as the love of God for him. That gave him the strength, even under persecution, to live in that grace and love. In Psalm 85 verse 10 we find these wonderful words, 'Love and faithfulness meet together; righteousness and peace kiss each other'. This is the character of God. They sum up for me the God I am coming to know. Even when I make mistakes, and I will - just as a child beginning to walk falls down - the important thing is to get up again, and to remember that I am declared righteous in His eyes because I have believed in the One who died for me. Where sin abounds, grace abounds all the more.

'The law was given through Moses, grace and truth was given through Jesus Christ.' (John 1:17) We needed the law to show up the difference between right and wrong, good and bad, but we could not keep the law with all its regulations. That is why God sent His Son to die for us and reveal His grace and truth that is available to all those who believe. It is now up to us to begin to live in that grace with the help of the Holy Spirit.

I returned from the bookshop with a bag filled with every book I could find on grace. I devoured every book drinking gallons of coffee, even reading some of them twice. As I began to understand a little more of what grace was, I wondered what book in the bible shows a group of people who were caught up, like me, in living by rules and trying to appease the gods.

In my search I turned to Paul's letter to the Galatians and read these words, 'I am astonished that you are so quickly deserting the one who called you by the grace of Christ and are turning to a different gospel.' (Galatians 1:6) What was that different gospel? It was a non-gospel - a religion of living by rules and regulations, not a gospel of good news.

I read on: 'You foolish Galatians, who has bewitched you? Before your very eyes Jesus Christ was clearly portrayed as crucified. I would like to learn just one thing from you. Did you receive the Spirit by observing the law or by believing what you heard?' (Galatians 3:1) For a year I studied this book of Paul's writing. I even bought Martin Luther's commentary on Galatians. I thoroughly enjoyed the study until I came to those words in chapter 3 verse 26, 'You are all sons of God through faith in Christ Jesus'.

It was this verse that threw me into confusion. How could I be a son of God? It was not a gender issue.

The issue was that there is only one Son of God and that is Jesus Christ. I believe the Bible to be the true inspired Word of God, but I could not understand this. After some time, I finished my study and laid the book aside, but I could not grasp the fact that I was a son of God until I understood the implications for my life.

Now I get it!

Back to that evening in TAFC. James Jordan continued his teaching on the glorious freedom that we can have when we know that we are sons of God. My mind and my heart had been prepared for that moment. I was so excited. I was like a child catching a ball for the first time, yelling, 'I've got it, I've got it'. Have you ever watched a child in the park being the goalie at a children's football match and the delight when the opposing team kick the ball at his goal post and he catches it? Have you ever watched grown men at a football match when their team has the ball? They go absolutely mad and run around in circles with delight. That is what I was like. I am a bit more mature than the men, (well, maybe!). I didn't scream - but I ran, oh yes, I ran! I laid aside decorum and politeness and, if anyone had stood in my way, I would have knocked them down, because I wanted to get to the bookstore at the church before anyone else.

When I got there, I said, breathing heavily, 'If this sermon has been recorded, I want the first tape that's produced'. What difference did it make if I had the first tape or the last tape? None at all, except that, in my urgency to get it, I would get it first. Maybe the first tape would have a greater anointing than any of the others! How dumb we are sometimes. I still remember the look on the girl's face at the bookshop as she tried to take down my details.   What on earth has happened to her, I could hear her thinking?

I ran back to the meeting to find James going around the room praying for people so, surprise, surprise, I joined the line. When James came to me I found myself saying, 'I want this James, I really want this. I want to begin to live in the glorious freedom of the children of God'.   Up until that moment I would never have approached the visiting speaker, because, to my way of thinking, they are on a higher plane than ordinary people. Who cared about that now? My one and only desire was to get hold of this truth. It was more important to me than anything else, even more important than what anybody thought of me. Not James the speaker from the other side of the world, not the pastor John Arnott, no one.

I was beginning to understand that My Father is Almighty God so, when I said to James, 'I want this, I really want this' - which was really very silly because I had already received it! - my mind was reasoning that, if there was more of this understanding that I am a son of God, then I wanted it. Of course, there are always deeper things in God to discover. He laughed when I said that and he put out his hand to bless me and pray for me. He had not even touched me before the power of God came upon me and I was thrown back and landed on the floor. Wonderful though it was to be touched by God in that way, that wasn't what made the difference.   For a brief moment every cell in my body became alive.   I can't explain what it felt like, but one thing I know is that, once you experience what it's like to be totally alive, you don't want anything that has to do with death.   Not dead religion.   Not dead works. Nothing. Only one thing matters and that is to experience life.

That is why Jesus came, to give us life, life in all its fullness. I don't live my life as fully alive as I would like, but, when deadness comes, I recognize it much more quickly. From that moment on, without any processing or reasoning, the spirit of poverty left me. I have no wealth to speak of and I live on the edge of a council housing estate, but I am free from what had held me in bondage all those years. Over the years preceding 2003, I had been given much by a close friend, John, to help me do the work of the ministry - and I am so grateful to him - but the vice-like grip of a poverty spirit did not begin to leave until that day.

Free to Serve

After I realized that this spirit had left me, (I doubt it was actually a spirit. I think it was more a mindset.) I remembered a prophetic word from the year before at a prophetic school. A man called Ivan Allum said to me, 'I have a picture. I see you feeding all these people and the hand of the Lord is on you and the things that you do. He is happy with what you are doing. He says that your cupboards will never run empty.' When I received these words I held them close to my heart, but my faith level was not at that point where I could truly receive them, believe them or even live in them. It was certainly a true word to me because I did feed over 40 people in the course of a week. The gift of hospitality is a visible sign that a community is alive.

Now I really believe that God will give me enough to feed the hungry, not just physically, but the spiritually hungry as well. How can I not believe that He who fed the thousands with five loaves and two small fish can still do miracles through a son of God? We serve the resurrected Christ. He is alive and has not changed. He is the same yesterday, today and forever.

Finding Contentment

I have to be careful because I don't want to have the kind of heart that only wants the gifts of God more than God Himself. In his letter to the church in Philippi, while chained up in prison, Paul writes in chapter 4 that he has known what it is like to be in need and yet he has known what it is to have plenty. And then he says these incredible words, 'I have learned the secret of being content in any and every situation.'

What does that look like? I don't know. Paul was in prison, had been shipwrecked, beaten and flogged and yet he could say, 'I know what it is like to have contentment.' That is one of my desires, to live in contentment whatever the circumstances. Difficult to do, but Paul says, ' I can do everything through him who gives me strength.' We often take this verse out of context. Paul is saying here that he will be given the strength to have contentment whatever the circumstances in his life. We need that gift of contentment today as much as the Philippian church did twenty centuries ago.

The church in Philippi was under threat of persecution for believing that Jesus was Lord, not Caesar. Their taxes were so high that they barely had enough to live on. If they didn't have anything with which to pay their fees, they lost their land to the rulers. I wonder if Paul was overtaxed by the Roman Government for his tent making, and yet could still say, 'I have learned the secret of being content.'

Generosity and Justice

'Father, help us to learn to be content in whatever circumstances we find ourselves in.' That prayer does not mean we are content with injustice and that we are content when we see the poor go hungry and children being killed, and famine reaching gigantic proportions. We are to stand up for these and fight alongside the poor who have no strength to fight for themselves. We become a VOICE for those who have no VOICE.

I long for the day when the Church rises up to see the desperate need that is around us all the time. My prayer is that God would work within us so that we who have plenty will reach out to those who have not. However little we might have, it is much more than others on the other side of the world. Millions of people go hungry and millions have no clean drinking water. Jesus gave the people food and water and healed those who were sick, and we are called to be like Him.

It is really not so difficult, but we often spiritualise everything and pray, 'Lord, what do you want me to do'? His word is clear, 'Take care of the widow, the orphan, the fatherless and the alien in your land'. We can begin right here, right now. With God's help, we will do so. As we help those in need we will find that we are also helping ourselves. When we begin to be generous, we begin a homecoming deeper into God because He is abundantly generous and extravagantly kind.

By giving we become like Him, and our orphan ways of focusing just on ourselves and fighting for what we feel we need, will begin to slip away. We will find that we will never walk alone. We will experience the reality that He will never leave us. He didn't leave us as orphans. He sent the Holy Spirit, the Comforter to be with us always. With His help we will give, because we can't help giving, not because we have to, but because our heart compels us. We will find that we are becoming a manifestation of Jesus in this world. As we give, we will find that the act of giving blesses us more than it blesses the one to whom we give. We don't know how that happens, it just does.

Reflection

1. Do you recognise the nearness of the Father who said that 'He will never leave you' a little more than you used to?

All that we receive from God is by faith. Ask Him right now that the seed of faith be planted in your heart so that it can begin to grow and you will come to find that He is loving you right now.

2. Do you recognise that, if He is loving you right now, you will never walk alone? May your spirit experience an awakening of this right now. Remember that He loves you and He is the Father you have been looking for all your life.

CHAPTER SEVEN
WE ARE FAMILY

God's Community Plan

As God is revealing Himself as Father, it is important for us to become family in the Body of Christ as the family of God, living community together.

Harold S. Kushner in his book 'To Life' says that 'one of the most important differences between Judaism and Christianity is that we [Jews] were a people before we had a religion'. He goes on to say that 'Christians form communities, but the faith commitment is always primary. But for Jews it is participation in the community that defines them'.

Rob Bell, Founding Pastor of Mars Hill Church in Grand Rapids, points out to us that, in the first three verses of Genesis God is revealed as a community of creativity: God as creator, the Spirit hovering, and the Word being spoken. My heart has always been for community without really having a language to describe it, so it excited me to find that before the beginning of time there is community in the very heart of God Himself.

As I look at what is happening among us at Citylife, I think about Harold Kushner: people come to us primarily not because of what we believe, but because they are looking for a family and a place of belonging, a place where their VOICE can be heard. We are becoming community. We are not a reformed community as some places say they have become, but a reforming community. To say we are a reformed community becomes a closed statement with no room for movement and change, but our world is always changing. Creation itself changes, season to season. I am happy to say 'reforming' because we haven't arrived - there is no arrival point anyway! - but we are beginning to see changes in the hearts of the people. Some people want to see greater changes and faster, but we are reaching a generation which has had no spiritual heritage for many generations. I am not in a hurry to see fast growth. James Jordan says that if you want to grow a cabbage, it doesn't take long; but if you want to grow an oak tree, it takes time.

Breakdown of Community

Much of our western society is disintegrating. There are few families who have both a father and a mother living at the same address with their children. Most of the children we minister to come from split homes. Marriage itself is a rare thing. We have a real love for our community. We visit the homes of all the children every week and so we become known, not only among the families we visit, but also in the area. At the shopping centre, I met one of the mums of a child who came to us. She asked, 'Helene, do you do weddings? I have been with my partner for eleven years and we would like to get married.' It was a great delight for me to conduct their wedding in their community and to see that they were willing to commit themselves to one another bringing a greater stability into their family life. Many from the community were there. It was a joyous day with a community of people celebrating together.

Some of the families we visit live in tenement blocks. They go home, close the door and shut themselves in. They become very private and struggle with isolation and loneliness. They don't want anyone to know their business. The underlying reason for shutting the world out is fear: fear of what people think of them and a basic fear of people in general. What people need is community, a place of belonging, a place of being accepted and loved for who they are so that the community can become a place of joy and freedom. Housing estates are filled with people who do not know one another. I suspect this is true about every city in the West. There is so much focus today on the individual. Even within the Church the focus is on the individual person. What does the bible say to me? What does God want me to do? We have lost the truth that it is about 'us' as a community or family of people helping one another and looking out for one another.

Since hearing the crying of the Fatherless during my visit to the Toronto Church, I have come to realise the incredible pain of isolation that is in the hearts of so many people. We were never meant to live like Robinson Crusoe on an island all on our own. Children have little to enrich their lives. Family breakdown means that they suffer incredible insecurity. They become rootless and have no idea what they want from life. As they grow up, their lives disintegrate and often find it impossible to connect with others, finding that they cannot put their roots down anywhere, or becoming unemployed because they don't know how to relate to other people.

The following article appeared on the BBC News Channel (Monday 1 December, 2008):

'The community life in Britain has weakened substantially over the past 30 years. According to a research commissioned by the BBC... a census reveals how neighbourhoods in every part of the U.K. have become more socially fragmented.'

They did a study to assess the health of a community by looking at how rooted people are in their neighbourhood. The article went on to say that Scotland's capital city tops the loneliness study. 'Edinburgh is the loneliest place to live in the UK according to a study commissioned by the BBC.' '33.1% of people in the area were less likely to be involved in their local community or to feel part of it'. '[Loneliness] has risen in Edinburgh by 13% since 1971 to overtake London and come top of the cities in the UK. In Scotland as a whole the figure for loneliness rose from 18.5% in 1971 to 28.5% in 2001'. This indicates that Edinburgh has worsened over the years.

Depression as one of the most crippling diseases of our time. An article on the internet states that 'depression in Scotland is a common medical condition, which often leads to intense feelings of sadness and despair and affects one in every five people at some time in their lives.' 'In Edinburgh and the Lothians it is one of the most common reasons for people to visit their GP, but it is estimated that as many as 75% of people with depression do not seek help from their doctor'.

However, I believe that when we begin to live community, when one is encouraged we can be a source of encouragement for those who that day feels low for whatever reason. The writer of Hebrews says that we are to encourage one another daily as long as it is called today. How much easier it is to do this while we live as community, as a family of God's people in relationship together.

It is very encouraging for us in Citylife to begin to see people having a place at college, getting a job or joining a club. Most of this is seen among people who have come to us for a long period of time. Without them realising it, it seems that stability is beginning to form in their lives. A routine or a rhythm is developing giving them a security and putting strength within them.

How did the Citylife Community begin?

About twenty years ago I was a counsellor at a Christian campaign. My role was, if someone responded to Jesus Christ, to draw alongside and ask if they had fully understood the commitment they had just undertaken. One of the people I drew alongside was an eight year old girl called Sarah. The campaign team were very keen on follow up and I was asked to visit the homes of every one I had counselled. I visited Sarah at her home in Broomhouse and her Mum was happy for me to do so. After a week or so Rosalind, her mum, asked me if I would take Sarah to the church that I attended. I was happy to take her because I was involved in the youth work.

I took Sarah and a few of her brothers and sisters along with a few other children who wanted to come, whose parents knew me. I ended up having eight children in my car and crying out to God, 'I shouldn't be doing this. It's illegal!' A short time later someone bought me an ex-council bright yellow mini bus that was falling to bits. It never started first time. The only way I could get the engine to kick in was to spray quick start on the mechanics and, because there was no lever to hold up the bonnet, I had to use the branch of a tree as a stick to hold it up. Then I used my spray, jumped in quickly, started the engine, jumped out, took away the branch and off we went.

Imagine this clapped out bus arriving at a church in a middle class part of town where most of the congregation were doctors, lawyers or professionals along with many university students. When we arrived, all the children jumped out. Children are not neat and tidy or quiet, so we totally disrupted the church. Over a period of time I began to realise that two cultures don't mix. How dumb was I – I had never thought it through. I tried to connect these youngsters into a church environment, but trying to make it come together made it too painful for everybody and so I had to look for another way. My heart was totally connected to these young people so when they went I had to go with them. At that time a new church had just been established in the city and I was asked to be the youth pastor.

Since I was now connected to the inner city through the visitation of the children and relationships with the parents I said to the church leadership that if they wanted me to do this I would disrupt their church. This was not deliberate, but what do you do with a nine year old boy who had witnessed his schizophrenic step father hold his mother by the neck and beat the living daylights out of her with his fists? It is totally impossible for him to sit still on a Sunday morning when the turmoil of the night before was churning around in his stomach. So he would run around the building with a leader, generally me, chasing him. He could not sit still. Sometimes I think we are expecting an outward behaviour to tow the line before the inner issues of the heart have been healed.

During this period of time the whole sense of community was touching us who were working with the young people at a deep level, and it seemed ridiculous to bus children into a city church when we wanted to affect an area. So with the blessing of the church, they released us and supported us for six months so that we could be established as a Ministry in our own right. That is how Citylife was birthed, with a small group of people, whose names are at the beginning of the book, whom I honour and to whom I owe my life. I honour their faithfulness to God and to one another to partner together to see His kingdom come in our little corner of the vineyard.

The Citylife Team

The Core Team in Citylife came about because we found that our hearts were knitted together. Our desire was to learn and grow together into a greater understanding of this God, who is mystery and yet relates to us as Father. To pray together, to cry together, to laugh together, to struggle together and work together with all our different personalities and different visions, but one thing held us together and that was a desire to see a new generation spring up, becoming healed and moving on with God in a changing world.

We were brought together by one desire – to know the One who is found in relationship and to make His VOICE known to the poor and disadvantaged. That desire brought us together to live a community life.

All God needs is that kind of desire in order to start revealing His infinite variety in each one of us and to bring that revelation to others so that truly we become like Jesus who said 'let your line shine' His light is within us to bring beauty and colour and harmony to the world. That brought us to the beginning of a journey together sharing together and receptive to the nudging of the Holy Spirit in our hearts. All we needed was a childlike faith with a sense of wonder and trust that takes the Presence and VOICE of God seriously in the choices that we had to take in our own lives and in every programme event that we put on in the work of Citylife. I realize that we do not work for God, but work with Him in what He is doing. It is so much easier when we work with our Father. It can become effortless for the bible teaches us that His heart has always been for the widow, the orphan and the outcast of society. Sometimes we get it wrong and then we become the saviour of the world and the burden becomes heavy. However, we have learned over the years that when it becomes heavy we are the ones who are carrying the load and not Jesus Christ.

One day I had a very scary experience when it was discovered that my husband had cancer. Mark, now on the Core Team of Citylife, had been reading the bible and God spoke to him about helping a widow. Now Mark did not know any widows, but he thought to himself, I know Helene and unless a miracle occurs she will soon be a widow as her husband is sick and has not been given long to live. The next day after God spoke to him, Mark phoned and said that he was sorry to hear the news and was there anything he could do. He thought I would respond to his kind request by asking him to change a light bulb. However, I said 'I would like to take you up on your offer, but what I need at this moment is someone to help me with the kids' work at church because Jim would need more of my help unless a miracle occurred and God healed him, and I wanted to be free to spend more time with him'.

Mark joined us all those years ago and he said jokingly one day that he had not realised it would be a long term commitment, so perhaps he should pray for a husband for me. I replied that we are called to pray a prayer of agreement and I would not agree to that as I don't know anyone who could handle the kind of life I lived. Over the course of the years we have become close friends. Within Citylife, apart from having a prophetic VOICE and serving on the leadership team, Mark has a strong desire to help people in decorating their houses and mending things that are broken. Through that he draws alongside them as they begin to open up to him. He doesn't look for a platform. I often wonder if in Christian ministry we are looking for a position and a role. Jesus did not elevate Himself. All He did was what His Father did.

I also believe that as we come together in relationship with God it is necessary to realize that it is not all about 'me'. It's about 'us'. The apostle Paul speaks in Philippians chapter 2 verse 12 about working out your own salvation. It seems that it is much easier to do this as part of a community. Paul wrote this letter to a community of believers in Philippi. He did not write it to an individual, and many people today, even although they profess faith in Jesus Christ, are not rooted and grounded in the love of God. While watching the film 'Shawshank Redemption' it became very clear to me what Paul meant in his letter when he says, 'Work out your own salvation with fear and trembling'. He meant that together we help one another to work out our salvation. In the film, one prisoner says that in the prison there is no such thing as hope, but the man who was doing a life sentence for a crime he had not done said, 'Hope is a good thing, perhaps even the best of things.' So when my hope is low I need to be around the people in the church community who have hope. When I have hope and others don't, they need to be around me. That way together we can work out our salvation.

Reflection

Are you part of a community of believers who can help you work out your own salvation? Do you feel that you are able to help others work out their own salvation?

If not, ask your Father to bring you into relationship within a community setting so that you can have a place of belonging for yourself, and to help others.

CHAPTER EIGHT
HEART FOR THE YOUNG

Faithfulness and Compassion

When did I first begin to have a heart for young people? I have been asked that question so many times. I remember as a child always dreaming of giving food parcels to the poor. I used to dream about it and my imagination ran with it. This vision began to take root in me while I attended a High English Church on the corner of my grandmother's street. I did not understand much, but I loved the liturgy and the smells of incense and something within the rhythm of the service touched my heart as I realised that I had so much while others had so little.

I think the outworking of this dream began when I was part of a youth group within the Church of Scotland who wanted to befriend children from a children's home. I was about sixteen years old at that time, and while that passion soon died, I learned early on that part of my character is stickability. Once I have said 'yes' to something I generally stick with it. At an early age faithfulness was becoming part of who I am. I believe God loves faithfulness in the heart of His people in response to His faithfulness to us. This puts stability into our lives especially in today's world of scattered people.

Scattered people are very evident within the housing estates. Part of our remit under God was to build relationships not just with the children, but with the parents and to be seen on the streets. We find that children we visit regularly are suddenly not there and their house is boarded up. They have moved to another area. Why? Perhaps they have developed bad relationships with their neighbours. Perhaps they built up debts they can't pay and move on to escape being caught. Perhaps it is just the desire for change. Whatever the reason, there seems to be within our culture generally an inability to focus and develop whatever is within us. One family I know has moved 17 times within 16 years. We now have a little ceremony in Citylife to give them a bag of groceries to bless their new home and we pray that it would become a place of belonging for them.

How many of us as children have started a new fad and only two months later it died. I remember my younger brother wanting to join a judo class. The outfit was bought only to find that within two weeks he didn't want to go to the classes any more. The outfit remained in the box.

People are looking for a connectedness, a place where they can put their roots down. A place where they can take their shoes off and it feels like home. A place where they can have communion with others whether we realise it or not and this provides a meaning to life's journey.

Making Connections

Three times I have returned to my home to find my windows smashed or my car broken into. I have been laughed and jeered at, 'Here's the Church wifie'. I have been offered Methadone to drink instead of the sherry when I was part of the Church in the Grange, a suburban area of Edinburgh. The contrast in visiting homes in the Grange and in the Council Estates is vast. It is like the difference between chalk and cheese, black and white, tidiness and shambles. Yet the inner crying of the people is just the same. Does anyone really know my name?' Does anyone know I am here? Does anyone know I exist?

One day when visiting an area where some of the children come from, I heard a very curt voice say, 'You, I want to speak to you'. Oh, I thought, what's happened now? A woman said, 'I have been watching you for over a year when you come on your visits. I have been very suspicious of you'. 'Why' I asked in bewilderment. 'Well, she said, it seemed very strange to me that you visit here every week at 3.30 p.m. and every Sunday pick up the children in a double-decker bus at the local bus stop. You come every week and I have noticed how the children come to greet you and call you by name and even put their arms around you'. And then she said something that made my heart leap, 'I want my children to come too'.

Reaching people is not difficult. You just need to accept them as they are. One of the major problems within society and within the Church is that we are trying to do a job, and so we become like an organisation and not like Jesus. We come under the world's systems, not the kingdom of God.

When we started Citylife in 2000 I visited the local police because I felt it important to let them know what we were doing, and through that contact we became very linked to Derek Brown one of the Community

Police Officers. We began to meet on a regular basis and talk about the 'buzz' on the streets. One of my first impressions of Derek was, when we were doing our weekly visits, we saw Derek standing speaking to a young girl whom I also know. When we finished our visits to that area we found Derek still standing listening to what she had to say. She came from a family who were very needy and were on drugs. I was so impressed at the time that he was taking to listen to one person. We use many words in today's world, but I have found that very few listen to what is being said. Very few are actually present to the person with whom they are having a conversation.

One day Derek visited me unexpectedly at my home and asked to speak to me. He had not come on business but to talk about his own life's struggles. For a couple of hours we just chatted and he left by thanking me for listening and he said 'I came to you because the team in Citylife are just like Jesus. Jesus did not sit in a building, but walked about the streets with the people'.

A few months ago I met him for a coffee and we started to chat together about what had been happening, not just on the streets, but what was happening in our own lives. He told me something very important which I have never forgotten. He said 'I am thinking of taking early retirement'. I was so surprised because he is so fit and healthy, and such a gift to the community. When I asked him why, he said that the police had become an organization, so that when he visited people to help them, they say, 'You have to do this. It's not as though you really like us. It's your job'. Derek was devastated and naturally so. He became part of the community because of his love for the people and his desire to see them change. Now it had become an organization and the people knew it. They had stopped confiding in him because it was his job. The Church can be like that if we run it under the world's systems of projects and administration. These are necessary and important but, the problem comes when we start 'doing' Church instead of 'being' Church. Before you know it, administration runs the Church and everything has to fit in with the project instead of the project being the outworking of what God told us to do.

People in the inner city are afraid of people in authority because of the problems they have experienced with people in authority in their childhood. I can understand this because of my own struggle with the authority my father had in our family. He was not abusive in any way, but he carried an air of authority that, if truth to tell, was a bit scary. He loved us in his own way, but he loved us more when we were well behaved and put on an outward act of discipline so that the neighbours and the people in his work would say, 'What well behaved children Alex has'.

One day I had a visit from a police official because he wanted to talk to me about a family that was connected to Citylife. One young lady was in my house at the time doing some paper work for me, and she was terrified. Why? He was very smartly dressed, highly polished shoes and carried a briefcase. He looked very official. Poor man it was not his fault that people are frightened of him. We spoke together for over an hour because of a situation that had developed within a family. This family had been visited on occasions by social workers and they would not let them in. Naturally they were afraid, because they as children had been involved with social workers and they carried an air of officialdom which instilled fear in them. At the end of our conversation he put down his pen and paper and turned to me and said, 'I don't understand this. How can you get into families homes when the social workers can't'? 'It is really simple,' I said. 'I like them'. I went on, 'You have come here to talk to me and you look very smart, very official, and that is not wrong. But circumstances that happen to us in our childhood affect us today. If I had not been healed of a relationship with my own father's authority in my life, you would have terrified me. But you don't. I can accept you just for who you are.'

Love casts out Fear

I realized then, in a very real way, by allowing the love of our heavenly Father into my heart, the fear of anyone in authority had disappeared. In 1 John 4 we read that it is perfect love that casts away fear. The more we allow the revelation of the love of God as a Father into our heart to heal us from past pain, the more fear slips away. I used to believe that fear was a spirit and that it should be cast out. I don't believe that now. I remember being at a Fatherheart Gathering when I experienced something I had never experienced before. It is something that is difficult to explain. Suffice it to say, it was like love came into the room. Now I know that not everyone experienced this, but to me it was real, so real that if I put out my hand I could touch it, but I could not do it. I could not stretch out my hand because this love was too holy. One thing I know is that love is 'stuff'. It is a substance. The book of Hebrews speaks of faith being a substance. I believe that, but I also believe that love is a substance and when His love is poured into our heart it changes everything.

When you have a care for people it flows through your life. We have been visited recently by a gang that roams around our area. They turn up at our building to try and cause trouble. However I have tried to draw alongside the leader of the gang and just chat to him. One day the gang turned up with some new members. One of the boys was being very difficult and was trying to get into the building to disrupt a meeting that was going on. He was quite 'high' on something and tried to be rude and aggressive, but the leader that I had come to know slightly, said, 'Don't you speak to her like that'. I was so pleased that he had accepted me. I would like to build up a greater relationship with him and his friends. Gangs are born because everyone needs to belong to some group or community. The ones in the gangs are just little boys and girls who need a place to belong.

Many people try to take authority in situations and rightly so but I have learned that if we go about saying we have authority – we don't have it. Authority is given by the people.

It really doesn't take much to diffuse situations, but you have to like the people and see them as made in the image of God however marred, and to look beneath the hardness of the masks and see with eyes of faith the beauty that is within each one of God's creation, remembering that God looked at the first man He made and said, 'That's very good'. I actually think He could have said, as a proud Father, 'Wow, that's real good'. I often have this image of our Father putting His arm around someone, calling all the angels over and saying to them, 'This is My son, isn't he handsome. I am so proud of him'. I remember saying that when I was ministering in Brazil when three young men who were deaf and dumb came up for prayer. I found myself saying to each one of them 'Our Father is so proud of you. You are His beloved son'. As I said this, my interpreter started crying. The lady who was doing the sign-language started crying. The three young men started crying and I started crying. He really is proud of His children and the walk they are taking.

I often imagine God putting His arm around a young girl and saying, 'This is My daughter, isn't she beautiful?' And all the angels go 'Wow!' I wonder if 'Wow' is used a lot in heaven. Only a three letter word, but it carries so much power.

Stability and Rhythm

We have so little connectedness and grounding that it seems we dislike anything that brings routine for our lives. As people come to Citylife on a regular basis, it puts stability into their lives. Our over stimulated society has also affected us in church circles. We want everything to be exciting in order that we can experience the next thrill. When we become over stimulated for a long period of time, we do not face the lostness, or the desolation that is often within us. We do not take time to face what is going on deep within our heart. The problem with over stimulation is that whatever we are involved in can have the veneer of success and it seems that we are moving in the favour of God. Perhaps that is so, but unless we come down from the high place and face what is going on inside of us, sometime or another we will crash or burnout or even move into sin because we want to live at that high and seek more and more to stimulate us.

In a way, I am learning to go back to my roots when I was a child of appreciating the richness of liturgy and having a rhythm of prayer and work in my own life. I am very comfortable in the Body of Christ. I love Charismatic meetings that have depth. I love Churches that preach the Word of God. I love the rhythm of Celtic spirituality. I love the Jesuit teachings and times of silence. I have spent time in Egypt where I took part in the Coptic services. I did not understand Arabic, but I began to get a feel for the rhythm of their services. For my own spiritual walk, I believe it is important to put in a rhythm of spirituality to ground us. This rhythm of prayer and work, and prayer and work and rest and relaxation should over the course of time become as easy as breathing. The 'in and out' breath of air that we live by is a rhythm to our bodies and to our lives which brings us in tune with creation itself, of which we are all part.

Start with One

So I stayed befriending children, and as my relationship with them deepened something was being birthed within me: to be used by God to bring healing and wholeness and a sense of self-worth to be planted deep within each child that God would put me in contact with over the course of the years. The deep longing intensified and only now are we beginning, in a small way, to see the fruit of that longing.

Often ministries or movements begin with one person. I believe it was Mother Theresa who, when asked how she coped with all the suffering in the world, she replied 'start with one'. I think that is so true. That is how I met Sarah.   To have a part in her walk has been a great privilege to me.   She is now grown up, married with three children and is Citylife's Project Worker and beginning to take a vital role in its ongoing work.   Her heart is very pastoral and has a real love and care for people.   I want the mantle that I have been given to be passed onto the next generation.

It has been exciting for us over the past years to begin to see what Malachi 3 prophesied: that the hearts of the children would be returned to the fathers and the hearts of the fathers be returned to the children. That is beginning to happen as a small group of families are coming along with their offspring.   This became very real to me about two years ago.   Sarah was sharing one Sunday evening and giving her testimony.   In the building were her whole family including her father, George. At the end of the meeting George asked to share and said that for the first time in two years he had spoken to his daughters. As he was sharing God spoke to my heart that this was the beginning of the first fruits of what Malachi had said.

Sarah's mother Rosalind has changed so much over the years that one day she arrived at my door with a bag of vegetables to make me a pot of soup.   She did this on a day when I was wondering, as we all do, 'Is this really worth it?'   God spoke to me and said, 'It is worth it, it really is.' Her whole family attend our fellowship, including her brother and sisters, one of whom is also on the Citylife team.   Her step-brothers also attend along with her father

Our role in Citylife is to help people on their journey and to perhaps find the path which is beneath every journey. I sometimes feel that we do not fully grasp the incredible privilege that we have in being invited into people's lives. Under the guise of Christianity there is often a great deal of criticism and harshness, but I believe we have to be invited to share in people's lives and earn the right to be heard.

In order to become known on the streets and by the children and the parents, we visit the homes of everyone every week. This has been a real blessing to us. When you visit a home for the first time, people are very suspicious of you. I understand that. After all, who are we? We need to earn the right to be heard. So every Wednesday at the same time we are in the area. We knock the door, say hello and chat for a moment. Over the course of the months, suddenly one day we are invited in. Over the course of the next few months we are asked for a cup of tea. Over the next few months people begin to open up and they begin to tell you about their lives. Then some time later we are asked questions like:

'My husband has gone away and hung himself, would you take the funeral?'

'One of our children has been abused, could you counsel them?'

'My child is being bullied. Can you pick them up to come to your group he is too afraid to come himself?'

Some years ago one of the children was killed in a hit and run and the family asked me to take the funeral. I suggested that they get someone from the local church, if they would like. However their reply really touched my heart. 'Oh no, you are the people who knew our son'.   Relationships are very important and it is wonderful when people begin to trust us and we are invited to take part in the most important aspects of their lives.

A 15 Year Journey

I have had the privilege of walking with one such person on her journey. Her name is Ashley.   I met Ashley when she was eight years old. She came from a broken and troubled family.   She was a very withdrawn child and it was difficult to get to know her.   Through her life she has had many ups and downs.   Broken relationships, two beautiful children to two different dads, one of whom spent some time in prison for violence.   But she kept coming to church.   She said it was the only place that she felt loved.   She met George, a lovely young man a year ago and he began to attend Church and has since become a Christian and he is a real joy to us. Over the next year we have watched them both develop and then six months later George asked Ashley publicly at church to marry him. I had the honour and privilege of marrying them the following September. On the Sunday evening just after the wedding Ashley asked to give her testimony.   She told it exactly as it had been for her, the pain, the mistakes and the struggles.   She said that she could not stop coming to Church even although her lifestyle was not right.   But she said that if she didn't come she might have turned to drugs.   She said something very interesting.   'When you have not experienced love, you look for it in all the wrong places'.   As she shared her story, the presence of God filled the room and there was a real tangible sense of His favour on her as she shared.   I believe that what happened for Ashley was that shame was taken from her and she could hold her head up. From the withdrawn girl of eight to the twenty three year old young woman of today who could speak with such clarity touched the whole meeting.

Sometimes when we have a dream which God begins to develop it within us. I know that often people want to do good for the poor and I bless them, because whoever gives a cup of cold water in Jesus' Name does it for Him. However, often it can be a duty and we obey the commandment. I have discovered that people aren't stupid, and my advice, for whatever it is worth, is don't do it unless you really like them. I remember a fourteen year old girl at the Wednesday Youth Group sharing after I had talked about the need to have love as a foundation in all our lives. If you want to build a house you need to put a strong foundation in to hold it. We will not grow or mature properly without that kind of foundation in our lives. I asked her if she had agreed with what I had spoken about, and she said 'Oh yes'. Then I asked her, 'How do you know somebody loves you'? She said, 'Oh, that's easy. You just look at their face'. If the love of God is not seen in us, it is absolutely useless. All our actions become like a clanging gong. What people are looking for is that we would be a manifestation of Jesus Christ wherever we go.

Waking up Sleeping Beauty

I would love to see community formed as a family, a place of belonging. A group of people who are rich or poor, educated or simple, young or old, healthy or sick. Together we would help one another grow and develop as people and help work out our own salvation. Mostly we minister with those who are less fortunate, those who are poor financially, emotionally, educationally and spiritually. I believe there is no such thing as a quick fix: healing and restoration are a process. Little by little we need to receive the milk of God's Word before we are able to eat the meat, the hard parts - that when we follow Jesus it can be difficult. However there is no other way to go.

We have had our spirits asleep for so long that we need an awakening. It's like Snow White in Sleeping Beauty who had been asleep for a long, long time until the Lover comes and he kisses her awake. I am discovering that underneath the abuse, verbal, physical or sexual lies the potential for greatness.

We in the Church have often tried to go out and do the works of Jesus. We pray, and fast and read the word, visit the prisoner, feed the hungry, pray for the sick and they are right to do because in my heart I want to be like Jesus. I did these things for years, but I wasn't becoming like Him. All I was doing was copying Him. I began to ponder, 'How did Jesus become like He was?' He didn't focus on Himself. He focused on His Father. In John's gospel Jesus said, 'The works that I do are not my works; they are the Father's living in me'. He also said that the words that He spoke were not His words but the Father's. In a very simple way it seems that in order to be like Jesus, our focus should be on the Father. May the cry of our heart be 'Father, help me to be like Your Son, that as we walk the streets of the land people would see Christ embodied in us, and be the manifestation of His Presence wherever we go. 'Father, please give to us a heart revelation of who you really are so that we can truly say that our Father just happens to be Almighty God.'

Reflection

What is the dream that God has placed in your heart? Has it been suffocated over the years? Has fear displaced love or will love displace the fear and liberate us to follow God's compassion?

CHAPTER NINE
AN INVITATION TO LEADERS

In these pages I have shared my own journey with my joys and my struggles, my successes and my failures, but all the time hoping to instil in us hope that, while there is no arrival point on this journey, there is a pathway leading us deeper into the heart of God.

All we need is the awareness that our Father is with us every step of the way, picking us up when we fall and encouraging us by saying to each one of us, 'Come on little one, we can do this together, let me take your hand.' We have to become like children utterly dependent on their Father. The grown up mature, got-it-altogether Christian has no need of a Father, or even of God, because his core belief is, 'I can do it all by myself'- just like Matthew as he used to go about singing 'All By Myself'. However, in reality we cannot do it by ourselves. We need the One who is greater than we are.

Here is a brief list of 'helps' that I have learned from Fatherheart Ministries, especially James and Denise Jordan, and others in the Body of Christ, who have helped me undergo a paradigm shift in my way of thinking and understanding.

Lesson One: Point to God and what God has done

One of the major lessons is not to tell people what they have to do or what they have to become. Our role is to tell them who God is and what He has done. It takes away the pressure of trying to make things happen and feeling a failure if people don't walk our walk. We are not the saviours of the world. Jesus Christ is. That takes a weight off our shoulders!

Christian ministry is about one thing: that is to bring people into the love of God found through a relationship with Jesus Christ. The bible teaches us that God is love. There are conditions to receiving the Father's love and provisions, but Jesus Christ has met them all. Can we begin to grasp this wonderful truth: 'Jesus Christ has met all the conditions' that God laid down? Love is not something you do, but something you have. It is shown when we begin to lay down our life for another. It shines out of our eyes as we walk the streets because our eyes are the windows of our soul. If we are full of the light and love of God it is seen in us.

Lesson Two: Focus on Freedom

In the western world, especially in Scotland, we focus so much on sin. We are told again and again that we are sinners, but God wants to bring us the glorious freedom of the sons of God. We become like the thing we focus on. The wrath of God is not God's punishment. Rather it is the experience of being left to our own devices when we choose to live a life without Him. If we focus instead on the freedom that God is bringing us into, thee we have to ask the question, 'what is freedom?' Freedom is lack of limitation because the essence of God's personality is that He is free.

The gifts of the Holy Spirit are marks of God's freedom. Manifestations in the Holy Spirit are evidence that God is among us. We are seeing the presence of God being revealed. The manifestations we experience are a physical reaction to His Presence. Since the eternal and the temporal cannot exist together, God turns up in a small way amongst His people revealing to us that He is alive and that we serve a resurrected Christ.

Prophecy, for example, is God speaking into our spirit. We pass it on because our human spirit can receive knowledge outside our senses. Our spirit picks it up as an impression, but our minds put it into words. Our mind then interprets what is in our spirit into the language we know. In the same way, healing is freedom from disease – a sign of God's free presence among us.

Lesson Three: Live as a Son not an Orphan

Trying to make ourselves holy and right, even as leaders in churches, can lead to self-righteousness; but to live like this is to live like an orphan, not as a son. An orphan sees God as a judge or a commander, someone who demands obedience. As a result, we try to fulfil the necessary commandments all on our own. As we force ourselves, and our congregations, into a daily discipline of devotion, we move into legalism. We have devotions for the simple reason that we are devoted to Him. We do not perform devotions out of a sense of duty, but because we want to devote ourselves more and more fully to the One who is devoted to us.

Obedience becomes an issue when we don't want to do what we are told and we end up obeying as an orphan. I know from other leaders in the Body of Christ that if we live like this we will experience burn out. Joy, peace and harmony with God disappear.

I have heard it said that 'your head is yours, but your heart is you'. Who we are in our hearts matters more than our intellectual understanding of who we are. Our heart is the seat of our emotions. It is who we are in the core of our being.

Orphans see the world an enemy environment and a dangerous place; but a son, moving in the revelation of God as Father, sees the world as his Father's world because the Kingdom of God belongs to them.

Orphan leadership demands submission and obedience, but you know when someone has true authority. One day I was getting on to the mini bus as some of the young people were being taken home after a meeting. As I jumped on to say goodbye to them, I heard one of the sixteen year olds shout to the other teenagers, 'Quick get your seat belt on, Helene's got on the bus'. I remember laughing because I had only gone to say goodbye. I realised later that I had authority because authority had been given to me by the people.

Jesus said, 'My sheep hear My VOICE and they follow Me.' Authority is seen and recognised by the followers, and people then have the choice to follow or not.

Orphan leaders are insecure because the love of the Father is not flowing through them, but a son loves to honour the Father. I value the Core Group in Citylife so much because we have come to love one another in a deep and real way. They honour me and I honour them, and, as we honour one another, people in our little family are beginning to love the people in leadership over them, because they feel safe. How healthy is that! An orphan spirit loves laws, but the only law we have is the law of love, and that knowledge of love gives peace to our hearts.

Lesson Four: Fathers and Sons

Our understanding of "covering" by leadership has taken the place of true spiritual fathering and mothering in the church. Our covering is family, not an organisation. A son draws spiritual fathering from someone who has had a revelation of the Father, and that leader may not even know that fathering is taking place. Spiritual fathering reveals a mature person who is walking with God. If you don't want to be a son, you will look for your own path and not even recognise a spiritual father when you see them. It is vitally important that we learn to have the heart of a son. That begins by having the heart of a son towards our earthly father and mother and then towards those in leadership over us. I am not talking about authoritarian leadership, but having the heart of a son towards the leader.

In Romans Chapter 8 we find that when we receive a spirit of sonship we can cry out 'Abba, father' because we find that the Spirit testifies to our spirit that we are God's children. Paul goes on in this chapter to speak of the adoption of sons. The Holy Spirit is the Spirit of the God who has brought us back from a far country into His country, but, even more amazingly, He has put His own Spirit within us. It seems that we are even more than adopted children because we have His Spirit. We share the same essence. The very seed of His life has been put into us. In 2 Peter chapter 1 we read that we are partakers of His divine nature which has been implanted in us. When we really get a handle on this truth, it changes everything.

I became very friendly with a family in a council housing estate that I have grown to love very much. Our love for each other has deepened over the years and they now see me as part of their family. I was invited to conduct both their daughters' marriages and it was a great honour and a privilege. I wonder if we really understand the privilege that we have to be invited into people's lives. We have no right to barge our way in. That is why I struggle with door-to-door evangelism (and I did it for years!). It just does not work except in the isolated case. I mention this family in particular because of what they have taught me over the years.

They had their two daughters, but they decided to foster children. Over the years John and Morag have fostered – wait for it......seventy children! How awesome is that! They also decided to adopt a boy when he was quite young whose family struggled to keep him. I was chatting to him one day (he is now eighteen years of age) and he said that there was often a little part of him that felt he did not quite belong. When I looked at the teaching in the Scriptures about having a spirit of adoption, I understood why this young man felt the way he did. His adopted mother and father love him passionately and so do his sisters and he knows that. He even said to me he would like to be like his adopted dad when he is a man. He does not see himself as adopted and neither does anyone in the family. And yet, in spite of all this, there are times when he feels isolated and not connected.

We are not only adopted at sons of God – we share the very Spirit of sonship.

Lesson Five: Decision-Making

If you are looking for a perfect church, or a perfect leader, or even a perfect congregation, you will not find one. We are a all wounded people seeking healing in our hearts through the only One who can minister that to us fully. However, you have to come to the place where you can trust older brothers and sisters in the Body of Christ to make decisions. If you are in a church and something goes wrong with a member of the congregation or even in the leadership, the entire church does not have the right to know someone else's sin or issue.

The Kingdom of God has a King, but the world has democracy. Democracy is the best way to govern this world's system. Within a democracy people have the right to know everything, but every person within a church does not need to know everything that the leaders are thinking and praying about. There is a place and a time when leaders will communicate with the members of the congregation about issues that affect and concern them, but there will always be some things that the leadership have to keep to themselves for reasons of safety and because some people within the congregation may not have the maturity to understand. If the church is a democracy it will only grow as fast as its least mature member. As leaders decide how much the people need to know and how much they can handle, trust is built up.

Lesson Six: Receivers First

The churches that are most alive are where leaders are first out at an altar call for prayer. To be an effective leader you need to be able to open your heart to receiving, first of all from God, but also from someone else, because have no redeeming qualities in ourselves. Jesus alone is our Redeemer.

Jesus is extending an invitation to all of us to become more vulnerable and not as guarded, to come to the place where we admit our struggles and our weaknesses. He also is waiting for an invitation from us to come into our places of abandonment and loneliness so that He can introduce us in a real way to our Father so that the Father's love can be poured into our spirit. The call of God on our lives is to be like His Son. I remind myself on a daily basis of what that call is, and seek a greater understanding that my Father loves me right now.

Not only did He love me when I was created, or even when I was being planned before the foundations of the earth, or even when His Son died for me, but His love is a present reality, right here, right now, within whatever circumstances I find myself. Jesus came because He loves us, but His primary reason was that He wanted to please His Father.

Over the years the church has focused on Jesus, and I understand that, but to become like Jesus I have found that I need to focus on the One that Jesus focused on. His focus was not on Himself, but on His Father. In John's gospel chapter 14, he speaks of himself, 'I am the way, the truth and the life'. For most of Christendom we have focused on this part of the verse, but we forget to really take hold of the rest ... 'no one comes to the Father except through Me'. The primary reason that Jesus came was to reveal the Father and to bring us to His Father. At the culmination of all things the Kingdom will be handed over by Jesus Christ to the Father. All of Scripture is about a Father who lost His kids and wants them back.

I extend an invitation to all who are reading this to 'Come' to Him. His hand is outstretched towards you and He bids you to 'come'. He really is the Father you have been looking for all your lives. He is the One in whose presence all fear is gone. The only requirement for us to enter in is to become a little boy or girl who needs to be loved.

Lesson Seven: The Way of Forgiveness

In order to enter more fully into the experience of the heart of the Father it is essential to walk the way of forgiveness. It is imperative that we forgive those who have wronged us especially our earthly father and mother. The bible says that unless we forgive from the heart God cannot forgive us. Many have made a decision to forgive, but it has been a choice, a mental decision which does not really free us. It is extremely difficult for many people to travel this road of forgiveness, especially those who have been abused sexually or physically. I remember hearing of someone who was abused by her father on a regular basis all throughout her childhood years. All the time he was abusing her he was reciting the Lord's Prayer and singing Christian hymns, and yet, with the help of God, she was able to release and forgive her father and come into a relationship with God Himself as her Father. How incredible is that! What courage it took for her to face this.

In order to fully forgive it is important to look at what was stolen from us. For some it was their childhood and for others it could be our innocence, but it will be different for each one of us. All of us have been hurt. It is important to take time out and look at what has been taken away and ask God to help us face these things. We may need someone that we can trust to help us work these things through, but it is important to get to the place that we can let them go through the way of heart forgiveness.

For myself I had to go through this way of releasing and forgiving my father for being an absent father, even although it was not his fault, and also for being authoritarian. I would like at this stage to point out that our parents - and others in authority over us - can only give to us what they have first received themselves.

Lesson Eight: Embrace Suffering

Often our cry to God has been, 'Why did you have to let this happen to me?' I do not have all the answers to this question, but I do know that to enjoy, and even to begin this life fully, means being able to embrace suffering, learning how to handle suffering without being embittered and all knotted up inside. It is so easy for us to become victims, but a victim can find their identity in being a victim. When we live life as a victim we are not living in the freedom that Jesus came to bring. Have you ever wondered how free Jesus was? He was free from the natural elements of this world. He could walk on the water. He could feed thousands of people. He could walk through walls after His resurrection. He could still the storm. He could even pay His taxes when He sent His disciples to find the money in a fish. I still wonder where that coin came from because I know that God does not deal in counterfeit!

I would like to finish by asking you to read a hymn I discovered, but have never heard sung. It is was written in 1866 by Annie Flint. Annie lost both her parents in childhood and then lost her foster parents.

She struggled with chronic arthritis most of her life so that even walking became difficult. The pen she used for writing was pushed between swollen, bent fingers and yet she could write this hymn. When life gets tough, and I feel I cannot go on any more, I read this hymn and reflect on it. It always encourages me to get up and go on. I invite you to join me in this meditation.

He giveth more grace when the burdens grow greater
He giveth more strength when the labours increase
To added affliction He addeth His mercy
To multiplied trials His multiplied peace.
Chorus:
His love has no limit, His grace has no measure
His power has no boundary known unto men
For out of His infinite riches in Jesus
He giveth, and giveth and giveth again.
When we have exhausted our store of endurance
When our strength has failed 'ere the day is half done
When we reach the end of our human resources
Our Father's full giving has only begun.
May we come to that place of faith and love and trust in God our Father, believing that for us His full giving has only begun. There is more to come. Hallelujah!

About the Author

Helene King lives in Edinburgh, UK and pastors an inner-city youth and children's ministry and emerging church. From a young age she has had a desire to share God's hope and compassion with children and young people. For the past 20 years this has been her primary focus and in 2001 she founded Citylife youth and children's ministry based in the west of Edinburgh.

Many years ago she received a revelation of God's amazing love which transformed her and her image of God. She takes God's message of unconditional love and grace out on to the streets in which she works and longs to see reconciliation amongst broken families.

Helene lives life to the full, she has an energy, enthusiasm and sense of adventure that touches all she meets.

She is an inspirational character, extremely generous with both her time and resources.

In her spare time she enjoys peace and quiet in her caravan by the sea and good coffee!

She is on the core group of Fatherheart Ministries which seeks to bring a revelation of the love of God as Father all over the world.

Fiona Cain, Director - Citylife

Lightning Source UK Ltd.
Milton Keynes UK
UKHW041320080119
335162UK00001B/17/P